マハトマ・ガンジーの霊言

戦争・平和・宗教・そして人類の未来

Spiritual Interview with Mahatma Gandhi

RYUHO OKAWA
大川隆法

本霊言は、2016年8月20日、幸福の科学 特別説法堂にて、
公開収録された(写真上・下)。

マハトマ・ガンジーの霊言
戦争・平和・宗教・そして人類の未来

Spiritual Interview with Mahatma Gandhi

Preface

Now, here is a hope for new world.

We need tolerance to love each other.

Patience is the essence of God's Love.

You, my neighbors and disciples.

Listen to me carefully.

"Love each other."

"Go beyond the wall of discrimination."

"Believe in God."

"Be merciful."

"Be kind to everything."

And,

"You shall see the kingdom of God."

Dec. 24, 2016

Master and CEO of Happy Science Group

Ryuho Okawa

はじめに

さあ、新世界への希望がここに示された。
互(たが)いに愛し合うためには寛容(かんよう)が必要なのだと。
忍耐こそ神の愛のエキスだ。
君よ、わが隣人(りんじん)にして弟子なる者たちよ。
わが言葉を心して聞くがよい。
「愛とは人と人との間に生じるもの。」
「差別の壁を乗り越えよ。」
「信仰こそ神。神こそ信仰。」
「慈悲(じひ)に徹(てっ)せよ。」
「天地万物(てんちばんぶつ)に心開(こころひら)くがよい。」
されば、
「君は、神の園(その)に座(ざ)している自分を知るだろう。」

2016 年 12 月 24 日
幸福(こうふく)の科学(かがく)グループ創始者兼総裁(そうししゃけんそうさい)
大川隆法(おおかわりゅうほう)

Contents

Preface 2

1 Summoning the Spirit of Mahatma Gandhi from Heaven 14

2 The Spirit of Gandhi Talks About the Truth of India's Independence 18

His aspiration came from inspiration from Heaven 20

The "only God" who created this world 24

Religious conflict between India and Pakistan 30

On the colonization by Britain 38

Indicating the aspiration for independence by only saying the truth 42

His understanding of Buddhism 46

3 Asking the Spirit of Gandhi the Problems in the Current World 52

Poverty itself is not justice 52

As for terrorism, "Be patient with each other" 62

God's philosophy is needed to overcome war 68

America should reflect on their use of nuclear weapons 72

目　次

はじめに ……………………………………………………… 3

1　天上界からマハトマ・ガンジー霊を招霊する ………… 15

2　ガンジー霊が語るインド独立の真実 …………………… 19

　　情熱のもとは天上界のインスピレーションだった …… 21
　　世界を創られた「唯一の神」……………………………… 25
　　インドとパキスタンの宗教対立について ……………… 31
　　イギリスによる植民地統治について …………………… 39
　　真実のみを語り、独立への悲願を示した ……………… 43

　　仏教に対する理解 ………………………………………… 47

3　ガンジー霊に聞く現代世界の諸問題 …………………… 53

　　貧しさそのものは正義ではない ………………………… 53
　　テロに関しては「互いに忍耐強くあれ」………………… 63
　　戦争を乗り越えるには「神の哲学」が必要 …………… 69
　　アメリカは核兵器の使用について反省すべき ………… 73

  His views on Japanese battles against western countries 78

  On North Korea's nuclear weapons development and China's territorial expansion 82

  Communism has been replaced by social welfare 86

  Hunger strike was "a deed of love" 92

  On Jainism's ahimsa and Islam's violence 96

4 A New World Religion that Can Overcome Discrimination 102

  Skin colors are different, but souls are not 102

  The one-god system and many-gods system are compatible 106

  Gandhi's soul has the mission to resolve racism 110

  His views on Donald Trump 120

  Why God created race 124

  Gandhi's message to the world 130

5 "Love Surpasses Hatred" Must be Our Main Aim 134

---

* This spiritual interview was conducted in English. The Japanese text is a translation added by the Happy Science International Editorial Division.

欧米に対する日本の戦いをどう見るか ……………… 79
　　「北朝鮮の核開発」と「中国の領土拡大」について ………… 83

　　共産主義は「社会福祉」にとって代わられた ……………… 87
　　ハンガーストライキは「愛に基づく行為」だった ………… 93
　　ジャイナ教的「不殺生」とイスラム教的「暴力」について … 97

4　差別を乗り越える新たな世界宗教 ……………… 103

　　肌の色は違っても魂に違いはない ……………… 103
　　「一神教」と「多神教」は両立できる ……………… 107
　　ガンジーの魂の使命は「人種差別の解決」……………… 111
　　ドナルド・トランプをどう見るか ……………… 121
　　神はなぜ人種を創られたのか ……………… 125
　　世界の人々へのメッセージ ……………… 131

5　「愛は憎しみを超えて」こそ目指すべきところ ……… 135

※本書は、英語で収録された霊言に和訳を付けたものです。

This book is the transcript of spiritual messages given by Mahatma Gandhi.

These spiritual messages were channeled through Ryuho Okawa. However, please note that because of his high level of enlightenment, his way of receiving spiritual messages is fundamentally different from other psychic mediums who undergo trances and are completely taken over by the spirits they are channeling.

It should be noted that these spiritual messages are opinions of the individual spirits and may contradict the ideas or teachings of the Happy Science Group.

本書は、マハトマ・ガンジーの霊言を収録したものである。
　「霊言現象」とは、あの世の霊存在の言葉を語り下ろす現象のことをいう。これは高度な悟りを開いた者に特有のものであり、「霊媒現象」（トランス状態になって意識を失い、霊が一方的にしゃべる現象）とは異なる。
　ただ、「霊言」は、あくまでも霊人の意見であり、幸福の科学グループとしての見解と矛盾する内容を含む場合がある点、付記しておきたい。

Spiritual Interview with Mahatma Gandhi

August 20, 2016 at Special Lecture Hall, Happy Science
Spiritual Interview with Mahatma Gandhi

マハトマ・ガンジーの霊言
戦争・平和・宗教・そして人類の未来

2016年8月20日　幸福の科学 特別説法堂にて
マハトマ・ガンジーの英語霊言　―戦争・平和・宗教、そして人類の未来―

Mohandas Karamchand Gandhi (1869 ~ 1948)

A politician and a spiritual leader of India. He was given the title Mahatma (great-soul) Gandhi, and is widely known as the great leader who guided India to independence. At the age of 18, he started training at the Inns of Court at Inner Temple in London. After he finished training, he opened a law office in Republic of South Africa and did activities to protect the legal rights of Indian immigrants. His thoughts were greatly influenced by the Hindu scripture *Bhagavad Gita* and Tolstoy. After returning to India, he did activities such as to boycott British products, the nation which colonized India, and set off the Salt March. These pacifist, nonviolent civil disobedience movements influenced the world greatly. India gained independence from the independence movement that took place after World War II. On January 30, 1948, Gandhi was assassinated, and a state funeral was held.

Interviewers from Happy Science

Kazuhiro Ichikawa
> Senior Managing Director
> Chief Director of International Headquarters

Yuta Okawa
> Managing Director, Deputy Chief of CEO's Office
> Religious Affairs Headquarters, Advisor of General Headquarters,
> Activity Promotion Strategist of Political Headquarters,
> Activity Promotion Strategist of International Headquarters

Masashi Ishikawa
> Director General of International Editorial Division

※ Interviewers are listed in the order that they appear in the transcript.
The professional titles represent the position at the time of the interview.

モハンダス・カラムチャンド・ガンジー（1869－1948）

インドの政治的・精神的指導者。マハトマ（偉大な魂）・ガンジーとも呼ばれ、「インド独立の父」として知られる。18歳でロンドンのインナー・テンプル法曹院に入学。卒業後は現在の南アフリカ共和国で弁護士を開業する傍ら、インド系移民の法的権利を擁護する活動も行った。インドの宗教叙事詩バガヴァッド・ギーターやトルストイ等に思想的影響を受ける。帰国後は、当時インドを植民地としていたイギリスの支配に対し、イギリス製品の不買運動や「塩の行進」など、非暴力・不服従の抵抗運動を行い、その平和主義的方法は世界に大きな影響を与えた。第二次世界大戦後の独立運動でインドは独立。1948年1月30日に暗殺され、国葬に処された。

質問者（幸福の科学）

市川和博（幸福の科学専務理事　兼　国際本部長）

大川裕太（幸福の科学常務理事　兼　宗務本部総裁室長代理　兼　総合本部アドバイザー　兼　政務本部活動推進参謀　兼　国際本部活動推進参謀）

石川雅士（国際編集局長）

※質問順。役職は収録当時のもの。

1 Summoning the Spirit of Mahatma Gandhi from Heaven

Ryuho Okawa We have a lot of members in India and all over the world. So today, I'll try to invite Mahatma Gandhi with English words from Heaven. It will be convenient for the people of the world.

About 20 years ago, or more than 30 years ago, I introduced through my spiritual message in Japanese and it's included in this *Okawa Ryuho Collections* (vol.10). But today, I'll try in English.

Mainly, we must ask him about war or peace, religion and future of the human race, or for example, about terrorism, or about the nuclear power or the nuclear attack, or invasion from the hegemonic countries. How does he think about them or the future of Asia, and future of the EU, the United States, Great Britain, or other countries? It depends on or it's up to your questions, so it's very important.

I'm trying to go to the New York session this

1 天上界からマハトマ・ガンジー霊を招霊する

大川隆法　私たち（幸福の科学）はインドや世界中に信者がたくさんいますので、今日は英語で、天上界からマハトマ・ガンジーを呼んでみたいと思います。そのほうが、世界の人たちにとっては都合がいいでしょう。

　20年ほど前、いえ、30年以上前でしょうか、日本語の霊言でガンジーをご紹介したことがあり、それはこの『大川隆法霊言全集』（第10巻）に収められていますが、今日は英語でやってみたいと思います。

　主として、戦争と平和、宗教、人類の未来について、あるいは、例えばテロリズム、原子力や核攻撃、覇権国による侵略などについて聞いてみないといけません。そういったことや、アジアの未来、ＥＵの未来、アメリカやイギリス、その他の国の未来について、ガンジーはどう考えているのか。あなたがたの質問にかかっていますので、非常に重要です。

　この秋はニューヨーク講演（注）に行く予定ですので、

autumn*, so this is also my rehabilitation [*laughs*] to speak in English. So I'm not so fluent, but please be patient and please keep silent and accept my words, word by word, carefully.

He, I mean Mr. Mahatma Gandhi, will not speak fluently through my mouth. So, I can just indicate the short conclusion regarding his will. It's not efficient or enough for all the people of the world, but we can appreciate, we will be able to appreciate his tendency regarding these political matters, around international politics, and about religion.

So then, let's start. Is it OK? All right.

Then, today, I will invite the spirit of Mahatma Gandhi of India. He is the great leader regarding the independence of India. Mr. Gandhiji, could you come down here? Gandhiji, Gandhiji, Gandhiji, Gandhiji, could you come down here? We'll invite you, seriously, respectfully. Would you come down here?

---

* On October 2, 2016, Master Okawa gave a lecture in English, "Freedom, Justice, and Happiness" at Crowne Plaza Times Square Manhattan in New York.

1　天上界からマハトマ・ガンジー霊を招霊する

　今回は私にとって、英語で話す〝リハビリ〟も兼ねています(笑)。それほど流暢には話せませんが、我慢していただき、静かに、一言一言、注意深く受け止めていただければと思います。

　マハトマ・ガンジー氏は、私の口を通すと流暢には話せないでしょうから、彼の念いに関して、短い結論を示すことしかできません。世界の人たちにとっては効率的でも十分でもないかもしれませんが、それらの政治問題、国際政治、宗教などに関するガンジーの考え方を理解することはできるかと思います。

　では、始めましょう。よろしいですか。はい。

　本日は、インドのマハトマ・ガンジーの霊をお招きいたします。インド独立の偉大な指導者でいらした方です。ガンジー先生、どうかご降臨ください。ガンジー先生、ガンジー先生、ガンジー先生、ガンジー先生、どうかご降臨ください。謹んでお招きいたします。ご降臨ください。

（注）2016年10月2日、大川総裁はアメリカ・ニューヨークのクラウン・プラザ・タイムズ・スクエア・マンハッタンにて、「Freedom, Justice, and Happiness」（自由、正義、そして幸福）と題し英語説法を行った。

2 The Spirit of Gandhi Talks About the Truth of India's Independence

Mahatma Gandhi [*Coughs.*] Hmm.

Kazuhiro Ichikawa Gandhiji? Mahatma Gandhiji?

Gandhi Yes, yes.

Ichikawa Today, we are so happy to welcome you.

Gandhi Oh, thank you. Thank you.

Ichikawa And we are so glad to ask you about the current world affairs.

Gandhi Oh, current affairs!? Oh, it's difficult for me. Ahaha, maybe.

2　ガンジー霊が語るインド独立の真実

マハトマ・ガンジー　（咳払い(せきばらい)）うーん。

市川和博　ガンジー先生でいらっしゃいますか。マハトマ・ガンジー先生でいらっしゃいますか。

ガンジー　はい、そうです。

市川　本日はお越しいただき、たいへん光栄に存じます。

ガンジー　ああ、ありがとう。ありがとう。

市川　世界の時事問題についてお伺(うかが)いすることができ、大変ありがたく存じます。

ガンジー　ああ、時事問題ですか。それは私には難しいかもしれませんね、ハハハ。

Ichikawa If it's possible.

Gandhi I'll try, but it's difficult because you are very intelligent. Intelligent people. So, it's very difficult for me. Please help me about comprehension of your question. I need your help to understand the current issue. OK?

His aspiration came from inspiration from Heaven

Ichikawa Before asking about the current issues, I have one question about when you were in India.

Gandhi India? OK.

Ichikawa You fought for the independence of India and fought against discrimination. So, what was your strong aspiration or motive or justice itself? What moved you to act strongly?

市川　もし、できましたら。

ガンジー　やってみますが、あなた方は大変頭がいい方たちですから、私には難しそうですね。ご質問の意味を理解できるよう力を貸していただけますか。時事問題を理解するうえで力を借りないといけませんが、よろしいですか。

情熱のもとは天上界のインスピレーションだった

市川　時事問題についてお伺いする前に、インドにいらした当時のことについて質問があります。

ガンジー　インドですか。どうぞ。

市川　あなたはインド独立のために戦い、差別と戦われましたが、あなたの非常に強い情熱、動機、正義とは、何だったのでしょうか。あなたを力強い活動に駆り立てたものは何だったのでしょうか。

Gandhi My aspiration came from inspiration from Heaven. So, it's almost the same as what you are doing, the mission of the hierarchy of the heavenly world. [*To Yuta Okawa.*] Do you want to ask me something?

Yuta Okawa Welcome to Happy Science.

Gandhi Oh, you're a good person and a young guy, a good young guy.

Yuta Okawa I think you mentioned what was important to you was Tolstoy's philosophy.

Gandhi Tolstoy's philosophy!?

Yuta Okawa Yes, and one of the Hindu bibles, *Bhagavad Gita**.

---

* One of the sacred scriptures of Hinduism that is set in a narrative framework of 700-verse of a dialogue between the prince and Krishna (incarnation of god). It is theorized that the date of its composition was from the 5th century to the 2nd century BC.

ガンジー　私の情熱のもとは、天上界のインスピレーションですよ。あなたがたが天上界の使命を果たしているのと同じようなものです。(大川裕太に)何かお聞きになりたいですか。

大川裕太　ようこそ、幸福の科学にお越しくださいました。

ガンジー　ああ、お若くて立派な方ですね。

大川裕太　あなたは、「自分にとって重要だったのは、トルストイの哲学である」と言われたことがあったと思います。

ガンジー　トルストイの哲学⁉

大川裕太　はい。そして、ヒンドゥー教典である『バガヴァッド・ギーター』(注)です。

(注)ヒンドゥー教の聖典のひとつで、王子とクリシュナ(神の化身)の対話形式による700行の韻文詩。成立時期は紀元前5世紀頃から紀元前2世紀頃までと考えられている。

Gandhi Hindu bible, of course.

Yuta Okawa Both two philosophies influenced you deeply.

Gandhi Not exactly. Of course, Hinduism is very influential to me, it's true. But Tolstoism is half and half. I influenced him and he influenced me. Yeah, both. We both influenced each other.

The "only God" who created this world

Yuta Okawa The activity of Satyagraha*, the disobedient and nonviolent activity.

Gandhi Yeah, it's a traditional Indian way.

---

* The term referred to the nonviolent civil disobedience movement developed by Gandhi.

ガンジー　ヒンドゥー教典ね、もちろんそうです。

大川裕太　その二つの哲学に、強く影響されたということでした。

ガンジー　正確に言うと少し違いますがね。ヒンドゥー教には当然、強い影響を受けましたが、トルストイ主義のほうは半々です。私が彼に影響を与え、彼も私に影響を与えたので、お互い影響を与え合ったということです。

世界を創られた「唯一の神」

大川裕太　サティヤーグラハ(注)、すなわち不服従・非暴力の活動についてはいかがでしょうか。

ガンジー　はい、それはインドの伝統的なやり方ですので。

(注) ガンジーが唱えた非暴力の抵抗運動のこと。

Yuta Okawa What was the historical source or just the source of such kind of thinking?

Gandhi God.

Yuta Okawa God?

Gandhi Just God. God's order.

Yuta Okawa What was the name of that God for you?

Gandhi It's a large print God.

Yuta Okawa OK. Is that the same as Hindu gods, or…

Gandhi I don't know exactly, but I think the Hindu god and the Jewish god and the Christian god and the Buddhist god or Buddha, I don't know exactly, and

　　　　　　　　　　2　ガンジー霊が語るインド独立の真実

大川裕太　そうした考え方は、歴史的に、あるいは歴史でなくても、どういったところから来ているのでしょうか。

ガンジー　神です。

大川裕太　神ですか。

ガンジー　まさに神ですよ。神の命(めい)です。

大川裕太　あなたにとって、その神は何というお名前でしたか。

ガンジー　大文字の「神(God)」です。

大川裕太　なるほど。ヒンドゥー教の神と同じ方ですか。それとも……。

ガンジー　はっきりとはわかりませんが、たぶん、ヒンドゥー教の神も、ユダヤ教の神も、キリスト教の神も、仏教の神あるいは仏も、はっきりとはわかりませんがイ

the Islamic god, all gods are one. If He created this world and if He created human beings, then He is the only God we can imagine.

Yuta Okawa I see. But for Indian people, there are a lot of names for gods…

Gandhi Ah, I mean… you mean…

Yuta Okawa Vishnu, or Krishna, or…

Gandhi …gods?

Yuta Okawa …gods, yes. So, for Indian people, it's a little bit hard to understand what you said. How can…

Gandhi Christian people don't know the large print God because priests of churches cannot explain about God. If you want to know God, you must love your

スラム教の神も、すべての神は、「一つ」なんです。神がこの世界を創られ、人類を創られたのなら、「唯一の神」であると想像がつきます。

大川裕太　わかりました。しかし、インドの人々にとっては、神の名はたくさんあり……。

ガンジー　ああ、つまり……。

大川裕太　ビシュヌですとか、クリシュナですとか……。

ガンジー　神々ですね。

大川裕太　はい、神々です。ですから、インドの人たちには、おっしゃることは少し理解しづらいと思うのですが。どう……。

ガンジー　キリスト教徒は〝大文字の神〟を知らないんですよ。教会の聖職者たちが神について説明することができないからです。神を知りたいのであれば、隣人を愛し、

neighbors, love other people, and love who hate you. At that time, you can understand the love of God and you can see the real magic of love and the real existence of God.

So now, one part of Christian people can understand what I say, but not all Christian people can understand what I say. They are attacking their enemies, so they cannot see any God, or a part of God, or they cannot hear the voice of God. So, it's a problem.

Religious conflict between India and Pakistan

Masashi Ishikawa I think you and Nehru* achieved the independence of India.

Gandhi Nehru? Nehru… OK.

Ishikawa Yeah, you and Prime Minister Nehru

---

* Jawaharlal Nehru (1889-1964) was the first prime minister of India.

人を愛し、自分を憎む者を愛さなくてはいけません。そうすれば神の愛を理解できますし、愛が持つ魔法のような力や、神の存在が、本当に見えてきます。

今、キリスト教徒のなかには、私の言っていることがわかる人もいますが、全員にはわかりません。彼らは敵を攻撃していますから、神の存在など垣間見ることすらできませんし、神の声を聞くことさえできません。そこが問題なわけです。

インドとパキスタンの宗教対立について

石川雅士　あなたとネルー(注)は、インドの独立を果たされたと思います。

ガンジー　ネルー？　ネルー……はい。

石川　はい。あなたとネルー首相はインドの独立を果た

(注) インドの初代首相ジャワハルラール・ネルー(1889-1964)。

achieved the independence of India and I think you two wanted one India.

Gandhi One India, yeah.

Ishikawa But unfortunately, it was divided into two countries, India and Pakistan. So, this is a religious conflict between Hinduism and Islam. And now, across the world, there are a lot of religious conflicts between Christianity and Islam. But you tried to integrate people as one. So, what do you think about…

Gandhi It's beyond my might. It's up to you. It's a future strategy for a new religion. We could not persuade each other, so it was my limit, but it was the limit of my age, I mean the era or the period of my living age. So, it depends on you. I think so.

Ishikawa I think at that time, there were lots of angels

し、お二人とも「統一インド」を望んでおられたと思います。

ガンジー 「統一インド」。そうです。

石川 しかし残念ながら、インドとパキスタンという二つの国に分かれてしまいましたので、これはヒンドゥー教とイスラム教の宗教対立です。また現在、世界中で、キリスト教とイスラム教の間に多くの宗教対立がありますが、あなたは人々を一つにまとめようとされました。ですから、どう思われますか……。

ガンジー それは私の力を超えています。あなたがたの仕事です。新しい宗教の「未来戦略」です。私たちは、お互いを説得できませんでしたので、それが私の限界でしたが、時代の限界だったんです。私が生きていた時代の限界でした。ですから、あなたがたにかかっていると思います。

石川 当時も、光の天使が数多くいたと思います。例えば、

of light, for example, Nelson Mandela, and I think you, too, when you were young, you went to South Africa.

Gandhi Yeah.

Ishikawa And at that time, you confronted racial discrimination.

Gandhi Yeah, of course.

Ishikawa For example, you had a first-class ticket, but the conductor told you to move to third-class.

Gandhi Yeah, yeah. Right, right.

Ishikawa So, that was maybe the starting point of your movement.

Gandhi But it's a small problem, it's not a problem,

ネルソン・マンデラもそうです。あなたも若い時、南アフリカに行かれたと思いますが。

ガンジー　はい。

石川　その時、人種差別に直面(ちょくめん)されました。

ガンジー　はい、もちろん。

石川　例えば、一等車のチケットがあったのに、車掌(しゃしょう)から三等の席に移れと言われました。

ガンジー　はい、はい。その通りです。

石川　それがあなたの運動の出発点だったのかもしれません。

ガンジー　まあ、小さな問題ですよ。小さな問題で、大

not so big of a problem.

Yuta Okawa As Marty (Ishikawa) mentioned now, in the time of the independence of India, during the process of separation, a lot of people were killed because of their infighting and, as you know, Islam is one of the most extreme or aggressive against evil things. Islam is such a religion, as you know. So, can your thinking of Satyagraha overcome Islamic philosophy?

Gandhi No, no, no, no, don't condemn Islamic people. They, of course, have some problems, but we, Indian people, also have a lot of problems. We have a caste system inside India. It means there are discriminations within India still now. We, ourselves, Indian people are Hindu believers. Even Hindu believers are in deep discriminations. We discriminate each other. So we, ourselves, cannot do the right things and have the right judgment, so we cannot have enough persuasion to Islamic people.

した問題ではありません。

大川裕太 今マーティ（石川）が触れたように、インド独立の際は、分離する過程で、内戦で多くの人が亡くなりました。また、ご存じの通り、イスラム教は、最も極端というか、悪に対して攻撃的な宗教の一つです。イスラム教はそういった宗教です。あなたのサティヤーグラハの考え方は、イスラム思想に勝てるのでしょうか。

ガンジー いえ、いえ、イスラム教徒を非難してはいけません。確かに、彼らにも問題はありますが、われわれインド人にもいろいろ問題はあります。インドは国内にカースト制があって、これは、インド国内にいまだに差別があることを意味しています。われわれインド人はヒンドゥー教徒ですが、ヒンドゥー教徒にも根深い人種差別があるわけです。ヒンドゥー教徒同士で差別しています。自分たちが正しいことができておらず、正しい判断ができていませんので、イスラム教徒に対して十分な説得などできません。

They believe in one God, Allah. They cannot believe in the Hindu gods. They discriminate us and we, Indian people, discriminate them. But we also have discrimination within our race, so we cannot condemn each other. We must forgive each other instead, I think so.

On the colonization by Britain

Yuta Okawa OK, thank you very much. You mentioned now about the caste system or Brahman system. During the age of colonization by England…

Gandhi Great Britain, you mean?

Yuta Okawa Yeah, Great Britain.

Gandhi Ah, OK, OK.

Yuta Okawa So, the caste system was originally a

彼らは唯一神アッラーを信じており、ヒンドゥー教の神々を信じることはできません。彼らは私たちを差別し、私たちインド人も彼らを差別していますが、インド人同士の間でも差別があるのです。ですから、互いに相手を非難することはできません。むしろ、互いに許し合わねばならないと思います。

イギリスによる植民地統治について

大川裕太　わかりました、ありがとうございます。今カースト制度、あるいはバラモン制度について話されましたが、イギリスの植民地時代に……。

ガンジー　大英帝国のことですか。

大川裕太　はい、大英帝国のことです。

ガンジー　ああ、はい、はい。

大川裕太　カースト制は本来、伝統的な制度でしたが、

traditional system. But Britain utilized that system in order to reinforce its colonization. They ruled India by using such systems. So, what did you finally think about the colonization by Britain?

Gandhi Ah, ha. Hmm… it's a very difficult matter. Great Britain had a great army, a huge army. We, Indian people, could not resist with weapons, so I chose to stand up for Indian people without weapons because if we used weapons, they would kill us more and more. So, it's ironical you may think, but if we don't use attacks or we use non-violent ways, our loss or our victims become fewer and fewer. So, it's our only way to resist with no violence and no obedience.

We just said, "You, the people of Great Britain, the people of England, have no power on us because this land doesn't belong to you. This is our land. You are intruders, so please get out from here." We just had such opinion and I imagined it would come true in the near future.

イギリスは植民地統治を強化するためにその制度を利用しました。そういう制度を使ってインドを統治しました。あなたは結局のところ、イギリスによる植民地統治についてどう思われていたのでしょうか。

ガンジー ああ。うーん……。実に難しい問題です。大英帝国には巨大な軍隊がありました。われわれインド人は武器では対抗できないので、私はインド人のために武器を持たずに立ち上がることを選びました。こちらが武器を使ったら、もっともっと多くの人が殺されていたでしょう。ですから、皮肉なことに思えるでしょうが、攻撃をしないで非暴力を用いれば、損失が、犠牲者数が少なくなるので、抵抗の手段としてはそうするしかなかったのです。非暴力、不服従です。

　ただ、こう言いました。「あなたがた英国民には、イギリス人には、われわれに関する何の権限もない。ここはあなたがたの土地ではないからだ。ここはわれらの土地である。あなたがたは侵略者である。出て行ってください」と。そうした意見を持っていて、近い将来、それが実現すると思っていました。

So, I obeyed my belief and the days followed my obedience, my belief. India received independence through our resistance. Nehru became the prime minister of India, and Jinnah* became the governor-general of Pakistan. It's sad for me, but it's beyond my power. So, it's sad but it's the job for the future people, I think.

Yuta Okawa Thank you very much.

Indicating the aspiration for independence by only saying the truth

Ishikawa During your movement, you had many supporters including international media from America or from the UK, so could you tell us the key to gaining support from many people? You used the

---

* Muhammad Ali Jinnah (1876-1948) is the founder and the first governor-general of Pakistan.

ですから私は自分の信念に従い、時代が私の信念についてきたわけです。インドは、私たちの抵抗運動を経て独立を得ることができました。ネルーがインドの首相になり、ジンナー(注)がパキスタンの総督になったのは残念でしたが、私の力を超えていました。残念ではありますが、未来の人たちがやるべき仕事だと思います。

大川裕太　ありがとうございました。

真実のみを語り、独立への悲願を示した

石川　運動期間を通して、あなたには多くの支持者があり、そのなかにはアメリカやイギリスのメディアもありました。多くの人の支持を得るための鍵とは何か、お話しいただけますでしょうか。言論の力やメディアの力を

　(注) 独立パキスタンの初代総督ムハンマド・アリー・ジンナー(1876 − 1948)。

power of speech or the power of media?

Gandhi Hmm. Newspaper. Maybe newspaper was very influential at that time. Now, you can use TV or the Internet or other tools, but at that time, newspaper was a great weapon for us.

Ishikawa Additionally, I think you also visited the UK and it was broadcasted through TV.

Gandhi But for British people, I was one of the poor people of India, so if they believed in me or not, I cannot guess, but I just thought that I must keep the truth and I just wanted to say the truth only. Nonviolence, non-resistance, non-obedience, and just indicate our aspiration for independence. That's all. That's all of my weapons. I don't understand the influence of my speech, but the age assisted me. I think so.

Ishikawa Thank you so much.

使われたのでしょうか。

ガンジー　うーん。「新聞」ですね。当時は新聞の影響力が大きかったかもしれません。今はテレビやインターネットや他のツールが使えますが、当時は新聞が大きな武器でした。

石川　それに加えて、あなたは英国を訪れ、それがテレビに映ったこともあったと思います。

ガンジー　ただ、イギリス人から見れば、私は一介の貧しいインド人でしたので、彼らに信じてもらえるかどうかわかりませんが、とにかく真実を守り、真実のみを語ろうとしたんです。非暴力、無抵抗、不服従、そして、ただただ独立への悲願を示すこと。それだけです。私の武器はそれだけでした。自分の言論の影響力についてはわかりかねますが、時代が私に味方してくれたのだと思います。

石川　ありがとうございます。

His understanding of Buddhism

Ichikawa Next question might be the last question about old India. When you lived at that time, there was a person named Dr. Bhimrao Ambedkar* in South India who was an activist and who…

Gandhi Recently?

Yuta Okawa Your age.

Ichikawa This person [*Shows the picture*].

Gandhi Ah, Ambedkar, Ambedkar.

仏教に対する理解

市川　昔のインドに関する質問は、次で最後になるかと思います。あなたのご生前、ビームラーオ・アンベードカル博士(注)という方がいらっしゃいました。南インドの活動家で……。

ガンジー　最近の方ですか。

大川裕太　あなたの時代です。

市川　この人物です(写真を見せる)。

ガンジー　ああ、アンベードカルね、アンベードカル。

---

* A politician and philosopher of India (1891-1956) (left photo). After India gained independence, he worked under the first prime minister of India Nehru as the law minister, helped architect the constitution of India and led the active movement against the caste system. In his later years, he converted to Buddhism and founded a new Buddhist movement.

（注）インドの政治家・思想家(1891-1956)。インド独立後に初代首相ネルーのもとで法務大臣を務め、インド憲法の草案作成に携わった。カースト制度の反対運動を指導。晩年仏教に改宗し、新仏教運動のきっかけとなった(写真)。

Ichikawa He's quite a famous neo-Buddhist leader in South India.

Gandhi Ah, OK, OK. I understand.

Ichikawa And now in South India, he is still quite popular. And he converted to Buddhism in 1956.

Gandhi Ah-ha. Neo-Buddhism?

Ichikawa Yes, Neo-Buddhist.

Gandhi OK.

Ichikawa How do you evaluate Dr. Ambedkar? He was a Dalit, but fought against discrimination and converted to Buddhism.

Gandhi Of course, I understand Buddhism and Gautama Siddhartha, Buddha, doesn't like

2　ガンジー霊が語るインド独立の真実

市川　南インドでは非常に有名な新仏教徒です。

ガンジー　ああ、はい、はい。わかりました。

市川　南インドでは、今でも非常に人気がある方です。1956年に、仏教に改宗しました。

ガンジー　ああ、新仏教ですね。

市川　はい、新仏教徒です。

ガンジー　わかりました。

市川　アンベードカル博士のことは、どう評価されますか。彼は不可触民でしたが差別と戦い、仏教に改宗したわけですが。

ガンジー　仏教については当然、理解していますし、ゴータマ・シッダールタ、仏陀が差別を好まないことも知っ

discrimination. His mainstream thinking is mercy and everyone can be maybe "small Buddha" through discipline and enlightenment. So, if he lived now, he would prohibit discrimination, I mean the caste system of India. His work was complementary activity for the independence of India, I think so. One of the good activities, I think so. But it's not everything. It's not everything. Yeah.

ています。彼の中心的な思想は慈悲であり、人は皆、修行や悟りによって、「小さな仏陀」になれるというものです。ですから、彼が今生きていたら、差別つまりインドのカースト制度を禁じたでしょうね。彼の仕事は、インド独立運動を補完する活動だったと思います。立派な活動の一つだとは思いますが、それがすべてではありません。すべてではないですね。

3 Asking the Spirit of Gandhi the Problems in the Current World

Ichikawa Thank you very much. So now, we would like to move on to world affairs.

Yuta Okawa Current affairs.

Gandhi Current affairs? Ah, it's a difficult one. Please assist me.

Poverty itself is not justice

Yuta Okawa So, firstly, I would like to ask you about wealth.

Gandhi Wealth?

Yuta Okawa Yes. You mentioned about poverty, but my image of you is that all the things you had

3　ガンジー霊に聞く現代世界の諸問題

市川　ありがとうございます。では次に、世界情勢に移りたいと思います。

大川裕太　時事問題です。

ガンジー　時事問題ですか。ああ、難しいところですね。力を貸してください。

貧しさそのものは正義ではない

大川裕太　まず、富についてお伺いしたいと思います。

ガンジー　富ですか。

大川裕太　はい。あなたは貧困について語られましたが、私が抱いているあなたのイメージは、持ち物は糸車(いとぐるま)とメ

were spinning wheels, glasses and clothes (photo below). Your image is 'very poor.' But as you know, the reason why Great Britain had great power was the accumulation of wealth. So, in today's world, wealthy countries govern this world and create rules in this world. What do you think about wealth?

Gandhi By nature, I was wealthy. And that's the reason I studied abroad in London, and majored in Law and became a lawyer. It depended on my wealth by nature, so I know the power of wealth.

ガネと衣類だけだったというものです(写真)。非常に貧しいイメージがあります。しかし、ご存じの通り、英国が強大な力を得たのは富の蓄積があったからです。現代では豊かな国が世界を支配し、世界のルールを決めています。富について、どのようにお考えですか。

ガンジー　私は、生まれは裕福だったんですよ。だからロンドンに留学して、法律を専攻して弁護士になれたんです。豊かに生まれついたおかげです。ですから富の力は知っています。

But at that time, almost all of the Indian people were poor, so we couldn't succeed in making money or social structures, like how Meiji Japan did. It's beyond my power, so it may be other people's great deed. Great businessmen should appear in India and they will make people happier through their money, I mean, prosperity.

But it's not my main point, so I think I did only politics through religious justice. That's my main work, so I don't think too much about how to make people rich.

Ishikawa Actually, top executives of American IT companies such as Google came from India, so I think they will return to India and they'll bring prosperity to India.

Gandhi India might be becoming a greater country in the meaning of capitalism. So, it's a good thing, but it's beyond my power.

ただ、当時のインドは貧しい人ばかりだったので、明治の日本がやったような「富」や「社会構造」の形成には成功しませんでした。それは私の力を超えていますので、別の人たちがやるべきことかもしれません。優れた企業家がインドに出るべきで、彼らが財力を通して、つまり繁栄を通して、人々を幸福にしてくれるでしょう。

　ただ、それは私の主目的ではなく、自分としては宗教的正義に基づく政治活動をしただけだと思っています。それが私の主な仕事ですので、人を経済的に豊かにするかどうかについては、あまり考えておりません。

石川　現に、グーグルなど、アメリカのIT企業のトップ経営者たちはインド出身です。彼らはインドに戻って、インドに繁栄をもたらすと思います。

ガンジー　今やインドは、資本主義の面で大国になりつつあるのかもしれません。それは結構なことですが、私の力を超えています。

3 Asking the Spirit of Gandhi the Problems in the Current World

Yuta Okawa And after your death, those who carried over your philosophy usually think of poverty as religious justice, for example Mother Teresa. I think she is kind of your friend in Heaven and such kind of philosophy is very popular in India. For example, the first Nobel prize economist of India, Amartya Sen, also stressed the importance of reducing economic injustice. But I think from the viewpoint of modern economy, to pursue prosperity...

Gandhi Pursue? What do you...

Yuta Okawa Pursue prosperity.

Gandhi Prosper?

Ichikawa Seek for prosperity.

Gandhi Ah, seek for. OK, OK.

3 ガンジー霊に聞く現代世界の諸問題

大川裕太　あなたが亡くなられたあと、あなたの思想を引き継いだ人たちは、貧困は宗教的正義であると考えるのが普通です。例えばマザー・テレサです。彼女は天上界であなたの友人のような関係だと思いますが、そういった思想がインドでは非常に人気があります。例えば、インドで初めてノーベル賞を受賞した経済学者のアマルティア・センも、経済的不正義を減少させることの重要性を強調しました。しかし、現代の経済の観点からは、繁栄を追求するためには……。

ガンジー　ツイキュウ？　それは……。

大川裕太　繁栄の追求です。

ガンジー　繁栄？

市川　繁栄を求めることです。

ガンジー　ああ、求めることですね。わかりました。

Yuta Okawa Seek for prosperity. Firstly, we are taught that to not have an allergy toward wealth is important.

Gandhi Allergy? Allergy. OK.

Yuta Okawa What do you think about that?

Gandhi Ah, OK, OK, OK. Poverty is not justice itself, I think so. Poverty is not justice, but being kind to poor people is justice. I think so. People must keep in mind that it's justice to be kind to poor people or miserable people and to save the miserable people and the poor people.

But poverty itself is not justice. Justice is not poverty. Please separate these two things because poor people are usually weaker people. Weaker people need help from others, other people in the world. Stronger people or wealthy people usually do good things for the poor. It's righteousness. It's justice, I guess so.

大川裕太 繁栄を求めるためには、まず、富に対してアレルギーを持たないことが大切だと私たちは教わっています。

ガンジー アレルギー？ アレルギーね、はい。

大川裕太 その点については、どう思われますか。

ガンジー ああ。はい、はい、わかりました。貧しさは正義そのものではないと思います。「貧しさ」が「正義」なのではなく、「貧しい人に親切にすること」が「正義」だと思います。「貧しい人、恵まれない人に親切にし、恵まれない人や貧しい人を救うことが正義である」ということは心に留めておく必要があります。

　しかし、貧しさそのものは「正義」ではありません。「正義」とは「貧しさ」ではありません。この二つを区別してください。貧しい人は、普通は弱者だからです。弱者は世の中の人から助けてもらう必要があります。強者や豊かな人が貧しい人に善行を施すのが普通です。それが正しいことであり、「正義」であると思いますね。

Yuta Okawa Thank you very much.

As for terrorism, "Be patient with each other"

Ishikawa I think the huge income gap leads to the rise of extremists or fundamentalists. For example, last year…

Gandhi Last year!?

Ishikawa I'm sorry, I'm sorry. Some Islamic extremist terrorists attacked the French newspaper *Charlie*…

Gandhi French newspaper?

Ishikawa Yeah, *Charlie Hebdo*⋆.

⋆ On January 7, 2015, a few armed Islamic extremists raided and opened fire at the Paris headquarters of *Charlie Hebdo*, a satirical weekly paper that published a controversial cartoon of Muhammad, and killed 12 editors and staff.

大川裕太　ありがとうございます。

テロに関しては「互いに忍耐強くあれ」

石川　収入格差が大きくなると、過激派や原理主義者の台頭につながると思います。例えば昨年……。

ガンジー　昨年ですか!?

石川　すみません、すみません。イスラム過激派のテロリストたちが、フランスの新聞社、シャルリー……。

ガンジー　フランスの新聞？

石川　はい、シャルリー・エブド(注)を襲撃しました。

（注）2015年1月7日、武装した複数のイスラム過激派が、ムハンマドを冒涜する風刺画を掲載した週刊紙「シャルリー・エブド」のパリ本社を襲撃し、編集者など12人を殺害した。

3 Asking the Spirit of Gandhi the Problems in the Current World

Gandhi Ah. Attacking. Terrorism?

Ishikawa Terrorism. Yeah, yeah.

Gandhi Islamic terrorism?

Ishikawa Yes, yes. How can we solve the issue of extremists or terrorists?

Gandhi Ah. It's very difficult. That's today's matter. It depends on Islamic people and depends on the thinking of people of the EU, so it's very difficult. It's beyond my power.

But I think being patient is very important. Of course, European people don't understand the real belief of the Islamic people, but Islamic people should not easily get angry and attack Christian people or people of the EU. It makes the flare of hatred.

So, I want to say, "Be patient with each other. Please keep calmness and become friends with other

ガンジー　ああ、襲撃ね。テロですね。

石川　テロです、はい、そうです。

ガンジー　イスラムのテロですね。

石川　はい、そうです。過激派やテロリストの問題は、どうすれば解決できるでしょうか。

ガンジー　ああ、それは実に難しいですね。今日的な問題です。イスラム教徒次第ですし、EUの人たちの考え方次第ですので、実に難しいことです。私の任を超えています。

　ただ、「忍耐」が大事だと思いますよ。確かに、ヨーロッパの人たちも実際のイスラム教徒の信仰を理解していませんが、イスラム教徒も、すぐに怒ってキリスト教徒やEUの人たちを攻撃したりすべきではありません。そんなことをすれば、憎しみの炎が燃え上がるばかりです。

　ですから、私は申し上げたい。「互いに忍耐強くありなさい。心の平静を保ち、他の人たち、無関心な人たちや

3 Asking the Spirit of Gandhi the Problems in the Current World

people or indifferent people or innocent people."

In religion, every believer who belongs to one religion is innocent to another religion, so we must think big and be kind to other people. Human nature, itself, is very good and sacred, so be kind to others and don't attack other people easily because it begins with innocence. So, "be patient." I want to say so.

Ishikawa Maybe most Western people tend to think the freedom of speech is more important than faith. What do you think about that?

Gandhi Sometimes I think so. I, myself, used the freedom of speech. Through the freedom of speech, I could make the independence of India. So, the freedom of speech and the freedom of paper, I mean broadcasting, is very important when we protest against the hegemonic empire. It's very, very, very important.

何も知らない人たちとも、仲良くしてください」と。

　宗教においては、ある宗教に属している信者は、他の宗教のことは知らないものなんです。ですから広い心で、人に優しくしなければいけません。人間の本質そのものは、「大いなる善」であり「聖なるもの」なのですから、人に優しくすることです。無闇に人を攻撃するのは無知から来ることなので、やってはいけません。ですから、「忍耐強くあれ」と申し上げたいと思います。

石川　欧米の人たちのほとんどは、「信仰より言論の自由の方が大切だ」と考えがちかもしれません。それについては、どうお考えですか。

ガンジー　私も、そう思うこともありますよ。私自身、「言論の自由」を行使しましたからね。「言論の自由」を通して、インドの独立を果たすことができたんです。ですから、覇権主義の帝国に対してプロテスト（抗議）するには、「言論の自由」「新聞の自由」「放送の自由」は非常に大切です。きわめて大切です。

But on the contrary, if people insist on their own discipline only, the freedom of speech sometimes makes hatred between people, so we must be careful about that.

God's philosophy is needed to overcome war

Yuta Okawa Thank you very much. So next, I'd like to ask you about war.

Gandhi War? Oh, war.

Yuta Okawa Yeah, in today's politics. You stressed the importance of nonviolence.

Gandhi Nonviolence, OK.

Yuta Okawa By thinking based on this philosophy, all kinds of war are not good. But today, in these days, for example, people in the United States tend to think

けれども逆に、自分たちの原則ばかり主張すると、言論の自由が人々の間に憎しみを生むこともありますので、その点は気をつけないといけませんね。

戦争を乗り越えるには「神の哲学」が必要

大川裕太　ありがとうございます。次に、戦争についてお伺いしたいと思います。

ガンジー　戦争？　ああ、戦争ですか。

大川裕太　はい。今日の政治における。あなたは非暴力の大切さを強調されました。

ガンジー　非暴力、はい。

大川裕太　その思想に基づいて考えれば、あらゆる戦争は良くないものです。しかし現代においては、例えばアメリカ人は、「良い戦争と悪い戦争がある」と考える傾向

there are good wars and bad wars.

Gandhi Good war and bad war.

Yuta Okawa War for justice is a good war. For example, to eliminate Nazism or fascism is a good war. But from your viewpoint, is there a good war or are there any wars which can be justified from the viewpoint of God?

Gandhi It depends. You mentioned about Nazism or Hitler's Germany, but at first we must think that German people are not such bad people. They are not evil by nature. So, they are also good people.

But when the government wants to have greater power than other countries, they sometimes destroy other civilizations, so this is a problem. Whether the civilization of that nation is greater than other nations

があります。

ガンジー　良い戦争と悪い戦争ですか。

大川裕太　「正義のための戦争は良い戦争である」と。例えば、「ナチズムやファシズムを排除するための戦争は良い戦争である」ということです。しかし、あなたからご覧になって、「良い戦争」というものはあるのでしょうか。あるいは、神の視点から見て正当化される戦争というものはあるのでしょうか。

ガンジー　場合によりますね。あなたはナチズム、つまりヒトラーのドイツに言及されましたが、まず、ドイツ人が特に悪いわけではないと思わなければいけません。生まれつき悪人というわけではなく、彼らだって良い人たちなんです。
　ところが、政府が他国に勝る力を持とうとすると、他の文明を破壊することがあります。問題はそこです。その国の文明が他の国より優れているか、あるいは他の文明より劣っているのか。それを判断し、理解し、決めるのは、非

or inferior to other civilizations, is very difficult to judge, understand or settle. It belongs to God. So, ordinary people, including me, cannot judge or justify the overdoing through war.

Every country thinks about the love for the world and the love for other nations and, of course, the love for their own country. We should integrate two types of love. For example, the love for Japan and the love for the United States, and we should integrate or envelop or accept these different concepts. It's a way to God, I think. Very difficult matter.

We need some kind of philosophy about that, but only God can explain the philosophy. So, it's very difficult for us to understand and we are entangled with the traditional thinking.

America should reflect on their use of nuclear weapons

Ishikawa I would like to ask about nuclear weapons.

常に難しいことです。それは「神の領域」です。私も含めて普通の人間には、戦争における行き過ぎた行為に関して判定したり正当化したりすることはできません。

どの国も、「世界を愛し、他の国々を愛する心」はありますが、当然、「自国に対する愛」もあるわけです。二つのタイプの愛を統合しなければいけません。例えば、「日本を愛する心」と「アメリカを愛する心」、この異なる考え方を統合し、包含し、受け入れることです。それが、神へと続く道だと思います。非常に難しい問題です。

ここに関しては何らかの哲学が必要ですが、その哲学を説明することができるのは、独(ひと)り神のみです。ですから私たちには非常に理解が困難で、伝統的な考え方にがんじがらめになってるんです。

アメリカは核兵器の使用について反省すべき

石川　核兵器についてお伺いしたいのですが。

Gandhi Uh-huh, nuclear weapons? Uh-huh.

Ishikawa Now, we have the problem of preemptive attacks by nuclear weapon. President Obama seems to refrain from using nuclear weapons, but what do you think about the world without nuclear weapons?

Gandhi Indian people already have nuclear weapons and Pakistan people already have nuclear weapons. They both are protecting their country. This is the reality. So, it's very difficult. If one country has nuclear weapons and another country… For example, "A" country dislikes "B" country and at that time, "A" country has nuclear weapons and "B" country doesn't have nuclear weapons. It means the tendency of the slaverism occuring from the lack of the balance of power. So, it's very difficult.

The United States… Mr. Barack Obama is a good person and a respectable person. So, if he says, "We won't use the nuclear weapon first," it's a good thing.

3　ガンジー霊に聞く現代世界の諸問題

ガンジー　ああ、核兵器ですか。はい。

石川　現在、核兵器による先制攻撃の問題があります。オバマ大統領は核兵器の使用を控えるようですが、「核兵器なき世界」については、どうお考えですか。

ガンジー　インド国民は、すでに核兵器を持っていますし、パキスタン国民もすでに核兵器を持っています。両方とも自国を防衛しているわけです。これが現実なので、非常に難しいですね。ある国が核兵器を保有していて、他の国が……。例えばＡ国がＢ国を嫌っていて、その時点でＡ国が核兵器を持ち、Ｂ国は核兵器を持っていなければ、パワーバランスが失われて奴隷的な傾向が生じることになります。非常に難しい問題です。

　アメリカのバラク・オバマさんは立派な方で、尊敬できる人物ですから、彼が「われわれは核による先制攻撃はしない」と言うなら、それは結構なことです。しかし

But before that, they should think about who used the nuclear weapon on this earth, Japan, Hiroshima and Nagasaki. Who destroyed these cities and who killed Japanese people?

If they reflect upon these things, they are entitled to say, "We must prohibit first attack of the nuclear weapons." But if there is no reflection about the attacking with nuclear weapons, it means there will be good wars and bad wars. So, if they think it's a good war, they can use nuclear weapon.

So, in general, if every country of the world prohibits using nuclear weapons, the people or the country that firstly used the nuclear weapon and threw it down on Hiroshima and Nagasaki should reflect upon the deeds. It's a beginning, I think so. American president cannot say that so easily. I think.

Ishikawa I think, at that time, President Truman called Japanese people, "They are like beasts."

その前に、地球上で核兵器を使用したのは誰なのか、考えてもらわなければいけません。日本の広島と長崎、これらの都市を破壊し、日本人を殺したのは誰なのか。

　彼らがこの点を反省するのであれば、「核による先制攻撃は禁じなければならない」と口にする資格があるでしょう。しかし、核兵器による攻撃について反省がなされないのであれば、「良い戦争」と「悪い戦争」があることになりますよね。それが「良い戦争」だと思えば、核兵器が使えるわけです。

　ですから、一般論として、世界各国が核兵器の使用を禁じるのであれば、広島と長崎に最初に核兵器を投下した国民ないし国は、その行為を反省すべきです。そこから始まると思います。アメリカ大統領がそれを口にするのは、そう簡単ではないでしょうね。

石川　当時トルーマン大統領は、日本人を、「彼らは獣(けもの)同然である」と称したと思います。

Gandhi Beasts?

Ishikawa Yeah, animals, not people.

Gandhi You are a beast. Oh [*laughs*].

Ishikawa Yeah, at that time. According to official…

Gandhi We are not beasts, we are slaves. Indian people are slaves. You are beasts. You are strong, so you are beasts. And we are weak, so we are slaves.

His views on Japanese battles against western countries

Ishikawa Do you think Japanese battles against western countries led to the elimination of racism and the liberation of colonies in Asia and Africa?

Gandhi I can't say exactly. We were under the control

ガンジー　獣ですか。

石川　はい、動物であって、人間ではないと。

ガンジー　獣ですか、ああ(笑)。

石川　はい、当時のことです。公式……。

ガンジー　私たちは獣じゃなくて奴隷(どれい)なんです。インド人は奴隷です。あなたがたは獣ですよ。強いから、獣なわけですね。私たちは弱いから奴隷なんです。

欧米に対する日本の戦いをどう見るか

石川　欧米に対する日本の戦いは、人種差別の撤廃(てっぱい)や、アジア、アフリカの植民地解放につながったと思われますか。

ガンジー　はっきりしたことは言えません。私たちは英

of the great empire of Britain, so we were a member of Great Britain at that time, so was it war of freedom or intrusion? We cannot say exactly.

I, myself, had been struggling about independence. But I didn't think that we'd invite other countries' violence, and we didn't plan to destroy the Great Empire of Britain through other countries' violence. It is not so fair, I think so. It's our matter within Great Britain. We must be independent, but we must resist by ourselves. So, the Japanese army attack… It was neutral for me. So, I cannot say it's good or evil exactly. You should ask for other great spirits' lectures. I think so.

Ishikawa Actually, Justice Pal* is very popular in Japan. He's from India. Thank you so much.

---

* Radhabinod Pal (1886-1967), an Indian jurist and judge. He served as one of the judges at the International Military Tribunal for the Far East, and is well-known for his *Dissentient Judgment of Justice Pal*, asserting that all of the defendants were not guilty.

国の支配下にあったので、当時は大英帝国の一員でした。ですから、あれが解放戦争だったのか侵略戦争だったのか、はっきりしたことは言えませんね。

 私自身は独立を目指して戦っていましたが、他国の武力を借りようとは思っていませんでしたし、他国の武力によって大英帝国を倒す計画もありませんでした。それは、あまりフェアであるとは思えませんね。自分たち大英帝国内の問題ですから。独立は果たさなければなりませんが、自分たちで抵抗するのでなければ駄目なんです。ですから、日本軍による攻撃は、私にとっては中立的です。その善悪について確かなことは言えません。他の高級霊にお訊きになったほうがいいと思います。

石川　実際、パール判事(注)は日本では非常に人気があります。インドの方ですよね。ありがとうございました。

（注）インドの法学者・裁判官、ラダビノード・パール(1886 - 1967)。極東国際軍事裁判で判事の一人を務め、被告人全員の無罪を主張した「パール判決書」で有名。

Gandhi Mr. Pal, ah. Mr. Pal, hmm. Yeah, some people wanted to make or build independence with Japanese military power, I think so. In some meaning, it's a good and smart thinking.

But in another meaning, Japanese army made a lot of massacres in the area of Asia, so it's very difficult to understand, I think. Mr. Pal is a good person and was the only friend of Japan at the end of WWII. But I do not have enough words about that.

On North Korea's nuclear weapons development and China's territorial expansion

Ichikawa About nuclear weapons, there is one nation. It's North Korea.

Gandhi North Korea?

Ichikawa It's like a brutal nation or immoral nation. They are developing nuclear weapons and they are

ガンジー パール氏、ああ、パール氏ね。そう、日本の軍事力を借りて独立したいと思った人もいたでしょう。ある意味で、名案であり頭がいいと思います。

ただ一方で、日本軍はアジアで多くの殺戮(さつりく)を犯したので、非常に理解が難しいところでしょうね。パール氏は立派な方ですし、第二次大戦終了時における日本の唯一の友人でした。ただ、その点に関しては、あまり申し上げることはできません。

「北朝鮮の核開発」と「中国の領土拡大」について

市川 核兵器に関しては、北朝鮮という国があります。

ガンジー 北朝鮮ですか。

市川 野蛮(やばん)でモラルのないような国です。彼らは核兵器を開発しており、日本に向けて弾道ミサイルを発射して

launching ballistic missiles toward Japan. So now, Japan is under the threat of North Korea. How do you see this kind of nation like North Korea?

China is expanding its territory in the South China Sea, and there are crucial disputes between China and Vietnam or the Philippines or Indonesia or other nations. How do you see these nations and how do we deal with these matters? What kind of future can you see in this area?

Gandhi It's very difficult, but I am not a professional war politician, so I don't have enough idea about that. But if I were Japanese, firstly, I would advocate that the United Nations should punish North Korea and delete North Korea. They are a UN member, I think, so they cannot keep that kind of quality or I mean that kind of pride for their country. They must be punished by the UN firstly.

And about China, if I were Japanese, the Japanese

いますので、日本は今、北朝鮮の脅威にさらされています。北朝鮮のような国をどのようにご覧になりますでしょうか。

　また、中国は南シナ海で領土を拡大しようとしており、ベトナムやフィリピン、インドネシアや他の国々と重大な論争が起きています。これらの国を、どうご覧になりますでしょうか。あるいは、こうした問題にどう取り組めばよいのでしょうか。この地域において、どのような未来が見えますでしょうか。

ガンジー　非常に難しいですが、私はプロの戦争政治家ではありませんので、それに関して十分な考えは持ち合わせておりません。ただ、もし私が日本人なら、まずは、「国連が北朝鮮を罰し、除名すべきである」と提唱しますね。北朝鮮は国連の加盟国だと思いますが、ああいった性質の傲慢な国でいてはいけません。まずは国連によって罰されるべきです。

　中国に関しては、もし私が日本人で、日本の首相か日

prime minister or Japanese religious leader, I would advocate, "Don't buy Chinese production. Stop their growth and stop the economic aid. Their military-first policy should be changed." If they change their mind, and if they choose disarmament, at that time, Japanese people would buy Chinese products and can invite Chinese people for such things. But now, Japanese government should prohibit or reduce buying Chinese goods. I think so.

Communism has been replaced by social welfare

Yuta Okawa Next, I'd like to ask you about communism.

Gandhi Communism?

Yuta Okawa I remember when you were alive, you felt a kind of sympathy for communism because in

本の宗教指導者なら、「中国製品を買うのはやめて、彼らの経済成長を止め、経済支援もやめて、彼らの先軍政策を変えさせるべきである」と提唱します。彼らが考え方を変えて軍備縮小を選択したあかつきには、日本人は中国製品を買い、そちら関係の中国人を招いてもいいでしょう。しかし今は、日本政府は中国製品の購入を禁止するか削減すべきだと思います。

共産主義は「社会福祉」にとって代わられた

大川裕太　次に、共産主義についてお伺いしたいと思います。

ガンジー　共産主義ですか。

大川裕太　私の記憶では、あなたは生前、共産主義に対し、ある種の共感を持たれていたと思います。共産主義は、

some aspect, communism assures the unification of a lot of peoples or nations.

Gandhi Ah, OK.

Yuta Okawa Certainly, for example, the Soviet Union or China has a lot of nations inside of its country and they could achieve the unification to some extent. But totally, communism is not so good from our Happy Science viewpoint. What do you think about this problem?

Gandhi Hmm. Communism can only spread poor countries. I think so. If its aim is to result in equality only, communism can only spread poor countries.

But if capitalism can make a growth for the country through freedom of market, there will appear a difference in incomes, of course, and the difference in success, I think. So, the countries of capitalism now are thinking about social welfare.

Social welfare problem or social welfare policy has

ある面で、多くの民族や国民の統一を掲げていますので。

ガンジー　ああ、はい。

大川裕太　確かに、例えばソ連や中国は内部に多くの民族を抱えており、ある程度、統一を果たすことができました。しかし全体としては、私たち幸福の科学の考え方からすれば、共産主義はあまり好ましくありません。この問題については、どうお考えですか。

ガンジー　うーん。共産主義は、貧しい国を広げるだけだと思いますね。「結果平等」を目指しているだけなら、共産主義は貧しい国を広げるだけです。

　しかし、自由市場に基づく資本主義によって国が成長したとしても、当然、収入格差や成功における差が生まれるでしょう。ですから資本主義国家は今、「社会福祉」を考えているわけです。

　近年は、社会福祉の問題、社会福祉政策が、共産主義

replaced communism in these years. So, the communism problem has already melted down. Communism is now a social welfare problem, I think so. In this dimension, there is no difference between communism and capitalism or communism and liberalism.

And even the advanced countries cannot be free from social welfare problem and the old age people's problem. So, these two trends, communism and capitalism, are making convergence these days, so it is just the difference in the way of explaining about what is wrong and what is bad, and what is right and what is justice. Just that kind of problem.

Even in India, we are becoming richer and richer and accumulated a lot of wealth, so there appears to be an imbalance between the poor and the rich people. So, next problem might be to minimize the difference of economic power or social welfare problem. No one can escape from this problem in this new world. I think so.

にとって代わっています。ですから共産主義の問題は、もはや消えてなくなりました。「共産主義」は今、「社会福祉問題」になっていると思います。この点で、共産主義と資本主義、共産主義と自由主義の間に、違いがなくなっています。

そして、先進国であっても、「社会福祉問題」と「老人問題」からは逃れられません。共産主義と資本主義という二つのトレンドは、現在は一つに収斂してきていますね。何が間違いであり悪なのか、何が正しくて正義なのかという、説明の仕方の違いに過ぎません。単にそういった問題なんです。

インドでさえ、どんどん豊かになってきていて、多くの富が蓄積され、貧しい人と豊かな人の不均衡が生じています。ですから次は、「経済力の差」や「社会福祉問題」を最小限に抑えるという問題が出てくるかもしれません。この新しい世界では、この問題から誰一人、逃れられないと思いますよ。

3 Asking the Spirit of Gandhi the Problems in the Current World

Yuta Okawa Thank you very much.

Hunger strike was "a deed of love"

Ishikawa We would like to overcome religious conflicts and racial discrimination and achieve a peaceful world through spreading universal Truth. And I think for example, you sometimes conducted a hunger strike to stop violence. So, what kind of qualities or mindsets are required to be a leader of peaceful movement or nonviolent movement to achieve a peaceful world?

Gandhi It's a traditional sect of Hinduism, you know, the Jain sect*, it's a brother religion of Buddhism. We sometimes make… You said hunger strike? [*Laughs.*]

---

* An Indian religion which was founded around the same time as Buddhism. The founder is Vardhamana (also known as Mahavira). Jains follow the principle of asceticism, and strictly practices the precept, *ahimsa* (nonviolence). Jainism was founded after the revolution of Nigantha sect established by Parshva.

3　ガンジー霊に聞く現代世界の諸問題

大川裕太　ありがとうございます。

ハンガーストライキは「愛に基づく行為」だった

石川　私たちは、普遍的な真理を広めることで、宗教的対立や人種差別を乗り越え、平和な世界を実現したいと考えています。あなたは、例えば、暴力をやめさせるためにハンガーストライキをされたこともあったと思いますが、平和な世界を実現するための平和的運動や非暴力運動のリーダーには、どういった資質や心構えが求められるのでしょうか。

ガンジー　あれは、ヒンドゥー教の伝統的な一宗派のジャイナ教(注)なんですよ。仏教の兄弟宗教です。私たちは、ときどき……「ハンガーストライキ」と言われましたか？（笑）

（注）仏教と同時期に成立したインドの宗教。開祖はヴァルダマーナ(尊称マハーヴィーラ)。苦行を重んじ、不殺生を徹底する厳格な戒律を守る。パーサが興した宗派であるニガンタ派の改革からジャイナ教が生まれたとされている。

Ishikawa [*Laughs.*] Yes.

Gandhi Hunger strike? Hmm... Ramadan-like strike in India. [*Laughs.*]

Ishikawa "I will not eat until the violence ends."

Gandhi Oh, yeah, yeah, yeah, yeah, yeah, yeah.

Ishikawa And recently, an American graduate student also did a hunger strike to eliminate racial discrimination at University of Missouri. I think it was inspired by you.

Gandhi It's a problem about love. We make hunger strike for the love of the people to stop attacking other people or to stop violence, at the price of my, or our lives. So, the followers or the friends changed their mindset and want to save me or person who made

石川（笑）　はい。

ガンジー　ハンガーストライキとは……うーん。インド流のラマダン的ストライキですかね（笑）。

石川　「暴力がなくなるまで食事をしない」という。

ガンジー　ああ、はい、はい、はい、はい、はい、はい。

石川　最近も、ミズーリ大学でアメリカの大学院生が、人種差別をなくすためにハンガーストライキを行いました。あなたに感化されたのではないかと思うのですが。

ガンジー　「愛の問題」なんですよ。ハンガーストライキは、人に対する攻撃をやめさせ、暴力をやめさせるため、人々への愛ゆえに、命がけでやるものなんです。それで、支援者たちや友人たちは考え方を変え、私やそうした行動に出た人たちの命を救おうとして、行動を慎み、暴力

such kind of conduct. So, they behave themselves and stop violence or too aggressive deeds. That's an aim.

It was the deed that I asked to stop making violence for other people. Please overcome your differences in opinions. For that meaning, I will give my life to stop the struggles, and it's my prayer for peace. If they understand me, I can live longer and longer. So, it is the deed of love, I think so.

Hunger strike does not sound so good. 'Fast' or another word can be replaced.

On Jainism's ahimsa and Islam's violence

Yuta Okawa Next, I'd like to ask you about a little bit minor question, about Indian religion. Some people point out that your philosophy is influenced by Jainism. And nonviolent philosophy is very similar to Jainism philosophy by Mahavira or Parshva or…

や攻撃的に過ぎる行為をやめるわけです。それが狙いなんです。

その行為の意味は、「人に暴力を振るうのをやめてください。どうか意見の違いを乗り越えてください。その意味で、争いを止めるためにこの命を差し出します」ということでした。〝平和を求める祈り〟だったんです。そこをわかってもらえれば、私はもっと生きられるわけです。ですから、愛に基づく行為だったと思っています。

「ハンガーストライキ」というのは聞こえがよくないので、「断食」とか、他の言葉で言い換えられますがね。

ジャイナ教的「不殺生」と
イスラム教的「暴力」について

大川裕太　次に、少しマイナーな質問ですが、インドの宗教についてお尋ねします。あなたの思想はジャイナ教に影響されていると指摘する人もいます。非暴力の思想は、マハーヴィーラーやパーサなどのジャイナ教思想とよく似ています。

Gandhi Yeah, yeah, yeah.

Yuta Okawa So, what do you think about Jainism?

Gandhi Its main point is, don't kill or let others lives be happy. Violence cannot produce happiness. And don't kill others if you want to be happy. If you were killed by others, you must be unhappy. So, if you would be unhappy, you should not do the same thing to others. It is the nonviolence policy or thought of Jainism. And the same thinking leads to Buddhism. Buddha thinks like that, I think so. So, Buddhism is also a peaceful religion. In modern times, I can't understand if it's a global religion or not.

But the status quo of Islamic power, the recent Islamic superpower, is very different from nonviolence policy or thinking. They use violence easily because the builder of the Islamic religion used violence. They made a lot of fights against their ancestors and they made independence through violence.

3　ガンジー霊に聞く現代世界の諸問題

ガンジー　はい、はい、はい。

大川裕太　ジャイナ教についてはどう思われますか。

ガンジー　ジャイナ教の要点は「不殺生(ふせっしょう)」であり、あるいは、他の生命に幸福になってもらうことです。暴力からは幸福は生まれません。そして、「自分が幸福になりたいなら、人を殺すなかれ。もし自分が殺されたら、不幸であろう。自分が不幸なら、人にも同じことをしてはならない」。これがジャイナ教の非暴力主義です。同じ考え方は仏教にも通じます。仏陀の考えも同様だと思います。ですから、仏教も平和的な宗教です。現代では、地球的宗教なのかどうかはわかりませんが。

　しかし、イスラム教勢力の現状は、最近のイスラム教の大きな勢力は、非暴力主義とは大きく異なります。彼らは簡単に暴力を用います。イスラム教の開祖が暴力を用いたからです。彼らは先行者たちと激しく戦い、暴力によって独立を果たしました。

In this meaning, the history of Islamic people are very akin to that of communism. Communists also think that their utopia, the communitarian, communism utopia brings with it the occurrence of violence, I mean the violence revolution. In this period, they can kill their enemies. Their violence revolution has legitimacy in communism. But I think it is the rudeness and it is merciless and it is not a high quality religion.

So, they should change their mind from the age of their founders. And the situations changed very much, so nowadays it's not so good to spread the violence revolution throughout the world. We have the same news through TV or the Internet or newspapers. So, we must not be separated. Instead of that, we must love each other.

この意味では、イスラム教徒の歴史は共産主義の歴史とよく似ています。共産主義者も、「共産主義的ユートピアは暴力行為、暴力革命によってもたらされる」と考えていて、それまでの期間は敵を殺しても構わないんです。共産主義では「暴力革命」に正当性があるのです。しかし、それは粗暴(そぼう)で無慈悲(むじひ)であり、高等宗教とは言えません。

　ですから、創始者たちの時代から考え方を変えないといけないんですよ。状況は大きく変わりましたので、現代では、「暴力革命」を世界に広げるのは決して望ましいことではありません。現代人はテレビやインターネットや新聞で同じニュースに触れていますので、互いを切り離してはいけないんです。むしろ、互いに愛し合わなければいけません。

4 A New World Religion that Can Overcome Discrimination

Skin colors are different, but souls are not

Yuta Okawa Thank you very much. Next may be the main question, but I'd like to ask you about today's racism. Your big theme was to overcome racial discrimination. Nowadays, not only in India but also in the United States and European countries, racism is one big theme. Nowadays, in the United States, Africans are sometimes killed by white or even African policemen. This is a hot topic even in the United States. What do you think about today's racism?

Gandhi Even the religious people don't understand the difference between souls and bodies. Their bodies are different. Their colors are different. But their souls are not different. Souls have no color.

4　差別を乗り越える新たな世界宗教

肌の色は違っても魂に違いはない

大川裕太　ありがとうございます。次はメインの質問になるかもしれません。今日の人種差別についてお尋ねしたいと思います。あなたの大きなテーマは「人種差別」を克服することでした。現在、インドばかりでなく、アメリカでもヨーロッパ諸国でも、人種差別が大きなテーマになっています。今のアメリカでは、アフリカ系の人が、白人警官や、ときにはアフリカ系の警官によっても殺害されることがあります。アメリカでも、これが大変、問題になっています。現代の人種差別について、どう思われますか。

ガンジー　宗教を信じる人たちにも、「魂」と「肉体」の違いがわかっておりません。肉体には違いがある。肌の色にも違いがある。しかし、魂には違いはないのです。魂には色はないんです。

People are reborn into this world through God's plan. I don't explain completely about that, but people who lived in the ancient age or recent period become souls in Heaven and are reborn again in this earthly world, and at that time, they live with their bodies. Their bodies sometimes are black, white, or yellow, but the souls have no color. So, this kind of discrimination depends on ignorance, I think. It's meaningless, I think. In the eyes of God, we are equal.

Ishikawa So, Christianity and Islam lack the information of the spiritual world. Do you mean we need a new religion with a lot of spiritual world information?

Gandhi It's good. Black people and white people are equal.

人は、神の計画によってこの世に生まれ変わってきます。それについて完璧(かんぺき)に説明し切ることはしませんが、古い時代や最近の時代に生きた人々が、天国で魂となり、そして再び地上界に生まれてくるのです。このときは肉体を持って生きるわけです。肉体は黒いときもあれば、白や黄色のこともありますが、魂には色はありません。ですから、そうした差別は無知に基づくものだと思います。無意味だと思います。神の目には、われらは平等なのです。

石川　つまり、キリスト教やイスラム教には霊界情報が欠けているので、霊界情報が豊富な新たな宗教が必要である、ということでしょうか。

ガンジー　それでいいんです。黒人も白人も平等なんです。

The one-god system and many-gods system are compatible

Ishikawa Additionally, I think in this world, there are two types of religion. One is that believers worship only one God, such as Christianity or Islam.

Gandhi OK, OK, OK.

Ishikawa And on the other hand, you know, like Hinduism or Japanese Shinto, they worship a lot of gods. So, there are two types of religion. How can we make a bridge between these two types of religion?

Gandhi It depends on the definition or how to explain about God. The meaning of god, it depends on this word. People use the word "god" in many meanings and there used to be one god of one nation, one tribe, or I mean, for example, Jewish god or Japanese god or English god or Philippine god or Hawaiian god or

「一神教」と「多神教」は両立できる

石川　それに加えて、世界には二つのタイプの宗教があると思います。一つはキリスト教やイスラム教のように、唯一の神を信仰するものです。

ガンジー　はい、はい、はい。

石川　他方で、ヒンドゥー教や日本神道のように、多くの神を信仰するものがあります。つまり、宗教に二つのタイプがあるわけですが、この二つのタイプの宗教の間を、どうやって橋渡しすればよいのでしょうか。

ガンジー　それは、神の定義あるいは、神をどう説明するかにかかっています。「神」という、この言葉の意味にかかっているのです。「神」という言葉はいろいろな意味で使われ、かつては、一つの国や一つの民族に一つの神がいました。つまり、例えばユダヤの神、日本の神、イギリスの神、フィリピンの神、ハワイの神などといった

like that.

This god cannot include all the nations of the world, so if this one god insisted that they should overcome and control all the world, if that nation intends to overcome and have influence over the world, in that time, there should occur a war. I think so. Another god will clash with them.

So, firstly, we must think that great God, Original God or Creator God is a different one. And every country, every nation has historical gods. Some sects choose one god of that nation and they propaganda that god as the greatest one. But it's misunderstood. So, please separate this one.

You, Happy Science, have such kind of tendency that the greatest God doesn't discriminate any nation, but the god of the nation loves only their nation or their tribe only. So, this is the starting point of discrimination and struggle or war, historically. We must learn this truth in the historical context and in the spiritual context now. It's very important.

具合ですね。

この「神」は、世界の民族すべてを包含することはできませんから、もし、こうした神の一体が、「自分たちが全世界を征服し、支配するべきである」と主張し、その国が世界を征服して影響力を振るおうと意図したなら、その時点で戦争になるでしょう。別の神が、彼らとぶつかるでしょう。

ですから、まずは、「偉大なる神、根本神、創造神は、それらとは別の存在である」と考えなければなりません。どの国にも、どの国民にも、歴史上の神々がいます。宗派によっては、その国の神の一体を選んで、「その神こそ最高神である」と言って布教するところもあるでしょう。しかし、それは誤解です。ぜひ、そこを区別してください。

あなたがた幸福の科学は、「最高神はどの国民も差別はしない」という考え方ですが、「民族神」は、自分たちの国民や自分たちの部族だけしか愛していません。ここが歴史上、差別や争いや戦争の始まりとなってきたのです。今こそ、歴史的観点においても霊的観点においても、この真実を学ばなければなりません。ここが非常に重要です。

You, only Happy Science, can explain the essence of old, ancient Hinduism. You can explain old, ancient Hinduism, remake its explanation and now in the 21st century, you can explain the many-gods system and how it has been brought up and many-gods system and one-god system are compatible. So, only you can explain this Truth. Only the right people who can understand the spiritual Truth can explain this Truth.

So, I expect much from Happy Science. You are the new Hinduism and you are the new Shintoism and you are the new Christianity and you are the new Judaism. So, you can overcome every discrimination and make a new world religion. I expect so much.

Gandhi's soul has the mission to resolve racism

Ichikawa Thank you very much. And as we are asking about spiritual matters, I'd like to ask about the world you are now in because it's been more than

あなたがた幸福の科学だけが、古い、古代のヒンドゥー教の本質を説明することができます。古代のヒンドゥー教を説明し、新たに説明し直し、今この21世紀において、「多神教」の成り立ちを説明でき、「多神教」と「一神教」がいかにして両立できるかを説明できるわけです。この真実を説明できるのは、あなたがただけです。霊的真実を理解することのできる正しい人だけが、この真実を説明することができるのです。

ですから、幸福の科学には大いに期待しています。あなたがたは〝新たなヒンドゥー教〟であり、〝新たな神道〟であり、〝新たなキリスト教〟であり、〝新たなユダヤ教〟であるんです。ですから、「あらゆる差別を乗り越えて、新たな世界宗教を創ることができる」わけです。大いに期待していますよ。

ガンジーの魂の使命は「人種差別の解決」

市川　ありがとうございます。霊的な内容を伺っておりますので、あなたが現在いらっしゃる世界についてお尋ねしたいと思います。あなたが地上を去り、あの世に行かれて

fifty years since you left this world to the other world. Perhaps in Heaven, you are proceeding some kind of sacred project or perhaps you are leading some people on earth. Is it possible to describe your sacred mission that you are conducting in Heaven? Or are there any people who you are guiding?

Yuta Okawa We got information from your guardian spirit several years ago. Your guardian spirit said his name is Manu*, the first son of man in Indian history.

Mythological picture of seven sages and Manu (back of the boat) surviving the Great Flood protected by the Fish God, an avatar of Vishnu.

七人の賢者とマヌ（船尾の人物）がヴィシュヌ神の化身の魚に守られ、大洪水を生き延びる神話の場面の絵。

から、50年以上経っていますので。たぶん天上界で、何か聖なるプロジェクトを進めておられたり、あるいは地上の人間を指導されていたりするかもしれません。そこで、あなたが天上界で担われている聖なる使命について、ご説明いただくことは可能でしょうか。あるいは、どなたか指導されている方はいらっしゃいますでしょうか。

大川裕太　数年前、あなたの守護霊様から得た情報があります。守護霊様は「マヌ」（注）と言う名を名乗られました。インド史で、人類の始祖とされている方です。現在、

★ In Indian mythology, it is taught that, as Manu is the son of the creator of the world, he is the "progenitor of mankind." At Happy Science, it has been revealed that Manu is an existence from the ninth dimension (a world of saviors where spirits that have evolved to their highest level as human beings reside) and Gandhi is the branch spirit of Manu (refer to *The Laws of the Sun* [New York: IRH Press, 2013], *The Nine Dimensions* [New York: IRH Press, 2012] and *Kamigami ga Kataru Remuria no Shinjitsu* [The Truth of Lemuria spoken by the gods] [Tokyo: IRH Press, 2010]).

（注）インド神話では、マヌは「世界の創造主の息子にして『人類の始祖』である」と伝えられている。幸福の科学は、マヌが九次元（人霊として最高度に進化した救世主の世界）存在であり、ガンジーはマヌの分身であることを明かしている（『太陽の法』『永遠の法』『神々が語るレムリアの真実』参照）。

So, how are you living in Heaven now?

Gandhi I'm just one person of India and a small human being and a small light of Heaven. So, don't respect me too much, I was a small person. You must respect upon your •Lord El Cantare. He will explain everything. I have a small power and I have a small mission, I have a small role. I just engaged in emancipation, I mean the freedom from racism nowadays. For example, South Africa, you know, Nelson Mandela or Priest King, Jr.

Ichikawa Martin Luther King, Jr.

Gandhi Yeah, yeah, yeah, yeah. For American freedom. And of course, not only my power, but also

---

●Lord El Cantare is the highest grand spirit of the terrestrial spirit group, and is a spirit from the ninth dimension which has been guiding humanity from the creation of Earth. He is the Supreme God of the Earth that Jesus called Father and Muhammad called Allah. A part of its core consciousness has descended to Earth as Master Ryuho Okawa.

4 差別を乗り越える新たな世界宗教

あなたは天上界で、どのように過ごしていらっしゃるのでしょうか。

ガンジー 私は一介のインド人であり、小さな人間であり、天上界の小さな光に過ぎませんので、あまり持ち上げないでください。小さな人間でしたので。尊敬すべきお方は、あなたがたの主エル・カンターレです。主はすべてを説かれます。私の力は小さく、使命も役割も小さなものです。ただ、解放に取り組んだというだけのことです。要するに、現代の「人種差別」からの自由ですね。例えば、あの、南アフリカのネルソン・マンデラとか、キング牧師とか。

市川 マーチン・ルーサー・キング・ジュニア博士ですね。

ガンジー そう、そう、そう、そう。アメリカの自由のためです。そしてもちろん、私は現在、自分の力だけで

●主エル・カンターレ 地球系霊団の最高大霊であり、地球の創世より人類を導いてきた九次元大霊。イエス・キリストが「父」と呼びムハンマドが「アッラー」と呼んだ地球の至高神である。その本体意識の一部が大川隆法総裁として下生している。

with other greater spirits power, I'm thinking about the immigration of the Arabic people to the EU. And I'm afraid of their future society. So, these problems of species and racism or discrimination, these matters are my main points, I think so. But the greater framework regarding the new religion, it depends on El Cantare.

Yuta Okawa Do you have a next plan to get a life on earth? Where do you expect to get a life in the future?

Gandhi Next, if possible, I can change the regime of China. If possible.

Yuta Okawa So, what kinds of activity will you do in China?

Gandhi Nonviolence. [*Laughs.*] [*Audience laugh.*]

Yuta Okawa OK. That's important.

はなく、もっと偉大な諸霊の力もお借りして、アラブ系の人たちの「EUへの移民」について考えているところです。彼らの社会が将来どうなるか心配ですからね。そういった「人種」や「人種差別」、「差別」の問題が、私の中心的な仕事かと思います。ただ、新たな宗教に関するもっと大きな枠組みは、エル・カンターレのお仕事です。

大川裕太　次に地上にお生まれになる計画はありますか。将来、どちらに生まれることをお望みでしょうか。

ガンジー　次は、できることなら中国の政治体制を変えてもいいですね。もしできることなら。

大川裕太　中国では、どういった活動をされますか。

ガンジー　非暴力です。（笑）（会場笑）

大川裕太　なるほど。それは重要ですね。

Gandhi No obedience. [*Laughs.*] And upset the government.

Ishikawa By the way, do you guide Malala Yousafzai?

Gandhi Ah, Malala. I know, I know. I know her.

Ishikawa Sometimes you give inspirations?

Gandhi She is going to be friends with Indian people and she wants to be a bridge between Pakistan and India. She's going to be a wall against religious violence and the discrimination regarding women. Men and women. It's her mission. She will be a new age Mother Teresa. I think so. I hope so.

ガンジー　不服従。(笑)そして政府を転覆(てんぷく)させます。

石川　ちなみに、マララ・ユスフザイさんはご指導されていますか。

ガンジー　ああ、マララね。知ってます。知ってますよ、彼女のことは。

石川　彼女にインスピレーションを送られたことはありますか。

ガンジー　彼女はインド人と仲良くなるでしょうし、パキスタンとインドの架(か)け橋(はし)になりたいと思っています。彼女は、宗教的暴力や、女性の、男女間の差別に対する、防波堤(ぼうはてい)になるでしょう。それが彼女の使命です。〝新時代のマザー・テレサ〟になってほしいですね。

His views on Donald Trump

Ishikawa This is a little difficult question. What do you think about Donald Trump?

Gandhi Donald Trump? America? American?

Ishikawa Yeah, the U.S. presidential candidate. He doesn't want Muslims to enter the United States until safety is assured.

Gandhi Hmm... He is a changeable person, I think. He battled with other candidates through TV shows, so he said too much about discrimination, but in his mind, he thinks another thing, I guess so. Now is August, and the election date is November. He will change, I think so. He will change and he will educate himself and will want to become the new president of the United States. He will educate himself and he is

ドナルド・トランプをどう見るか

石川　少し難しい質問なのですが。ドナルド・トランプについて、どう思われますか。

ガンジー　ドナルド・トランプ？　アメリカ、アメリカ人の？

石川　はい、アメリカ大統領候補の。彼は、安全が確保できるまではイスラム教徒を米国に入国させたくないと考えていますが。

ガンジー　うーん……。彼は変わる余地があると思いますよ。テレビで他の候補者たちと争っていたので、差別発言をし過ぎましたが、心の中では違う考えだと思います。今は8月で、選挙は11月でしたか。彼は変わるでしょう。考えを変えて、自分を教育し直して、合衆国の新大統領になろうとするでしょう。自己教育するでしょうし、頭のいい人ですから、変わると思います。

a smart man, smart guy and he will change, I think.

And of course, my soul tendency will be regarded as Mr. Obama-like tendency or Hillary Clinton's tendency. But for America, it is in one point, it's good, but in another point, bad. So, it depends on their fate and the fate of the world. And you are thinking from the problem of Japan. It's beyond my power, so I can't say definitely what is the good thing to do.

Mr. Donald Trump has a weapon in his mouth, but he sometimes says the correct thing and he speaks from the standpoint of world justice. It will change the Japanese mind and the Japanese tendency which relies

もちろん、私の魂の傾向性は、オバマさんやヒラリー・クリントンと同じだと見なされるでしょうが、それはアメリカにとって、いい点もあり悪い点もあります。彼らの運命と世界の運命次第です。あなたがたは、日本の問題から考えておられますがね。まあ、私の力を超えていますので、どうするのが良いか明確には言えません。

ドナルド・トランプ氏には「口」という武器があります。正しいことを言うときもありますし、世界的正義の観点から発言していますので、それを受けて日本人の考えが変わり、他国に頼りすぎる日本人の傾向性が変わること

In Jan. 2016, Master Ryuho Okawa recorded a spiritual message from the guardian spirit of Donald Trump. The day after Trump's campaign win on Nov. 10, Master Okawa gave an English lecture titled, "On Victory of Mr. Donald Trump" where he touched upon his predictions of America and the world under Trump's administration. [See *Trump Shin Daitouryo de Sekai wa Kou Ugoku* (Tokyo: IRH Press, 2016. English-Japanese bitext. Photo).]

大川隆法総裁は2016年1月、ドナルド・トランプの守護霊霊言を収録。同氏の大統領当選翌日の11月10日には英語説法「On Victory of Mr. Donald Trump」を行い、トランプ政権下のアメリカと世界に関する予測を述べた。『トランプ新大統領で世界はこう動く』(写真・幸福の科学出版刊、英日対訳)参照。

too much on another country.

Japan should establish her own will. It's a new age. It will start from next year. Japan will change. And the tendency of Japanese people of 71 years will change in the near future. You can be a brave nation and you can be a savior for other weaker countries. It's your samurai spirit. Your samurai spirit will be welcomed by other countries of Asia, I think so.

Why God created race

Yuta Okawa OK. May I ask a question? It's probably the last question from me. I heard from Master, you and your soul is in charge of racial problems in the Earth's history. You are from the ninth dimension*, a ninth dimensional spirit. You, Manu spirit is in charge of racial problems.

It's my question, why did El Cantare create 'race'

---

* See footnote on page 113.

になるでしょう。

　日本は自国の意志を確立すべきです。それが新時代です。来年から始まるでしょう。日本は変わりますよ。71年間続いた日本人の傾向性が近い将来、変わるでしょうね。日本は「勇気ある国」となることができます。力の弱い国々を救う〝救世主〟となることができます。それが「日本のサムライ精神」なんです。日本のサムライ精神が、アジアの国から歓迎されると思います。

神はなぜ人種を創られたのか

大川裕太　わかりました。質問してよろしいでしょうか。私からは最後の質問になると思います。総裁先生から、あなたとあなたの魂は、地球の歴史において人種問題を担当されていると伺っております。九次元（注）のご出身で、九次元霊でいらっしゃいます。あなた、つまりマヌの霊が人種問題を担当されています。

　そこで質問ですが、エル・カンターレは、なぜ「人種」

（注）p.113の注を参照。

and what was its purpose? There are a lot of races from the ancient times, from the beginning of the Earth. What was the purpose of El Cantare?

Gandhi [*Laughs.*] It's a difference of wearing… I mean the clothes. Your clothes are different because you have an identity. You have self-tendency. You have your own will, your own self-realization. This is the difference of colors and the differences of races, nations and countries. So, in some meaning, differences make conflicts, but in another meaning, differences make progress. So, that's the mind or intention of God, I guess so.

Yuta Okawa Thank you very much.

Ishikawa My last question.

Gandhi Uh-huh.

というものを創られたのでしょうか。その目的は何だったのでしょうか。太古から、地球の創世期から、いろいろな人種が存在しています。エル・カンターレの目的は何だったのでしょうか。

ガンジー （笑）それは、〝着ているもの〟の違い……〝服〟の違いですよ。みなさん、いろんなものを着ているのは、自分のアイデンティティがあるからでしょう。自分の傾向性がありますし、自分の意志があって、自分なりの自己実現がある。それが(肌の)色の違いであり、人種や国民や国の違いなんです。ある意味で、違いは「争い」を生みますが、別の意味では、違いが「発展」を生むんですね。それが神の御心であり、ご意図であると思われます。

大川裕太 ありがとうございます。

石川 私からの最後の質問です。

ガンジー はい。

4 A New World Religion that Can Overcome Discrimination

Ishikawa I would like to ask about the future of humankind. According to Bill Gates, the next big problem is the labor substitution. I mean, artificial intelligence will replace human beings. From the viewpoint of abilities, maybe human beings will be defeated by artificial intelligence. But you taught us about the importance of the soul. In modern society, we tend to forget the mind or soul. So, if you have some advice to future generations…

Gandhi Hmm… I, myself, led an ancient Indian style [*laughs*], so I have no words about that. Of course, the Indian future depends on A.I., artificial intelligence. And the Indian people are rich in mathematical ability, so it might be their future great points. But I don't have any words about that. I just want to say the origin of the soul and the original tendency of the soul and original hope of God. That is my mission.

So, please ask that question to Bill Gates or other great businessmen. I cannot answer about the relation

4　差別を乗り越える新たな世界宗教

石川　人類の未来についてお尋ねしたいと思います。ビル・ゲイツによれば、次に大きな問題となるのは「労働代替(だいたい)」です。要するに、人工知能が人間にとって替わるだろうということです。人間は、能力の点では人工知能にかなわないかもしれませんが、あなたは魂の大切さについて教えてくださいました。現代社会では「心」や「魂」が忘れられがちですので、未来の世代に対して何かアドバイスがございましたら……。

ガンジー　うーん……。私自身は古代インドのスタイルで(笑)やっていた人間ですので、それに関しては何とも言えませんね。もちろん、インドはこの先、AI、つまり人工知能に頼ることになりますし、インド人は数学が得意なので、そこが今後の強みになるかもしれませんが、私としては何とも言えません。私は「魂の起源(きげん)」や、「魂が本来持っている性質」や、「神の本(もと)なる願い」についてお伝えしたいだけです。それが私の使命なんです。

　ですからその質問は、ビル・ゲイツか、誰か優秀なビジネスマンの方に聞いていただけませんでしょうか。AI

between A.I. and human race. I cannot predict about that, so please ask that to such kind of future-oriented people.

Gandhi's message to the world

Ichikawa Thank you very much. The time is coming, so as closing words, it is highly appreciated if you could give your special message to the world even though… just any words are appreciated.

Gandhi OK.

    The people of the world, please love each other.
    Overcome the wall of discrimination
    And make your souls more transparent
    And please purify your sacred mission.
    You are the warriors of God.
    It means to fight against evils
    With love only.
    Mercy only.

と人類の関係については、お答えできかねます。予測は無理ですので、その方面の未来志向の方たちに聞いていただけますか。

世界の人々へのメッセージ

市川　ありがとうございました。お時間となりましたので、最後の締(し)めの言葉として、世界に向けた特別なメッセージを、どんなお言葉でも結構ですのでいただければ、たいへん有(あ)り難(がた)く存じます。

ガンジー　わかりました。
　世界の人々よ、どうか、互いに愛し合ってください。
　差別の壁を乗り越え
　自らの魂をいっそう透明なものとし
　どうか、自らの聖なる使命を浄化してください。
　あなたがたは、神の戦士です。
　すなわち、悪と戦ってください。
　ただ、愛の力によって。
　ただ、慈悲の力によって。

That's my last word.

Ichikawa Thank you very much.

Yuta Okawa & Ishikawa Thank you.

Ichikawa This concludes the spiritual message from Gandhi. Thank you very much.

Gandhi Thank you very much.

これが私からの最後の言葉です。

市川　ありがとうございました。

大川裕太＆石川　ありがとうございました。

市川　以上でガンジーの霊言を終了いたします。ありがとうございました。

ガンジー　ありがとうございました。

5 "Love Surpasses Hatred" Must be Our Main Aim

Ryuho Okawa [*Claps twice.*] He spoke a lot. Thank you very much, Mahatma Gandhi. My poor English will be understood by a lot of people of the world, so it's my pleasure to help other people and help other people understand our attitude toward discrimination and racism.

We are living in the world of love, and "Love Surpasses Hatred" must be our main aim. So, be patient and quietly hear the voices from Heaven. I hope so.

5 「愛は憎しみを超えて」こそ
　　目指すべきところ

大川隆法　（二回手を叩く）いろいろ話してくれましたね。マハトマ・ガンジーよ、ありがとうございました。私の拙い英語は、世界の多くの人に理解してもらえるでしょうから、人びとのお役に立ち、「人種差別」などの差別に対する私たちの姿勢を理解していただければ、うれしく思います。

　私たちが生きているのは、愛の世界です。「愛は憎しみを超えて」こそ、私たちの目指すところでなければなりません。ですから、忍耐強く、天の声に静かに耳を傾けてくださることを願っています。

『マハトマ・ガンジーの霊言
　戦争・平和・宗教・そして人類の未来』

大川隆法著作関連書籍

『大川隆法霊言全集第10巻』（宗教法人　幸福の科学刊）
『太陽の法』（幸福の科学出版刊）
『永遠の法』（同）
『神々が語るレムリアの真実』（同）

マハトマ・ガンジーの霊言
戦争・平和・宗教・そして人類の未来

2017年1月18日　初版第1刷

著　者　　　大　川　隆　法
発行所　　幸福の科学出版株式会社

〒107-0052　東京都港区赤坂2丁目10番14号
TEL(03) 5573-7700
http://www.irhpress.co.jp/

印刷・製本　　株式会社 研文社

落丁・乱丁本はおとりかえいたします
©Ryuho Okawa 2017. Printed in Japan. 検印省略
ISBN 978-4-86395-868-5 C0014
Photo：Dinodia Photo／アフロ

大川隆法ベストセラーズ・英語説法&世界の指導者の本心

トランプ新大統領で世界はこう動く

英語説法 日本語訳付き

日本とアメリカの信頼関係は、再び"世界の原動力"となる——。トランプ勝利を 2016 年 1 月時点で明言した著者が示す 2017 年以降の世界の見取り図。

1,500円

守護霊インタビュー ドナルド・トランプ アメリカ復活への戦略

英語霊言 日本語訳付き

次期アメリカ大統領を狙う不動産王の知られざる素顔とは？ 過激な発言を繰り返しても支持率トップを走る「ドナルド旋風」の秘密に迫る！

1,400円

ネルソン・マンデラ ラスト・メッセージ

英語霊言 日本語訳付き

人種差別と戦い、27年もの投獄に耐え、民族融和の理想を貫いた偉大なる指導者ネルソン・マンデラ。その「復活」のメッセージを全世界の人びとに！

1,400円

幸福の科学出版

大川隆法ベストセラーズ・世界の指導者の本心

アメリカ合衆国建国の父
ジョージ・ワシントンの霊言

人種差別問題、経済対策、そして対中・対露戦略——。初代大統領が考える、"強いアメリカ"復活の条件。

1,400円

キング牧師
天国からのメッセージ

アメリカの課題と夢

宗教対立とテロ、人種差別、貧困と移民問題、そして米大統領選の行方——。黒人解放運動に生涯を捧げたキング牧師から現代人へのメッセージ。

1,400円

マザー・テレサの
宗教観を伝える

神と信仰、この世と来世、そしてミッション

神の声を聞き、貧しい人びとを救うために、その生涯を捧げた高名な修道女マザー・テレサ——。いま、ふたたび「愛の言葉」を語りはじめる。

1,400円

※表示価格は本体価格(税別)です。

大川隆法ベストセラーズ・英語説法&世界の指導者の本心

Power to the Future
未来に力を

英語説法集 日本語訳付き

予断を許さない日本の国防危機。混迷を極める世界情勢の行方——。ワールド・ティーチャーが英語で語った、この国と世界の進むべき道とは。

1,400円

ドゥテルテ フィリピン大統領 守護霊メッセージ

英語霊言 日本語訳付き

南シナ海問題を占う上で重要な証言！ 反米親中は本心か——隠された本音とは？ いま話題の暴言大統領、その意外な素顔が明らかに。

1,400円

ヘンリー・キッシンジャー博士 7つの近未来予言

英語霊言 日本語訳付き

米大統領選、北朝鮮の核、米中覇権戦争、イスラム問題、EU危機など、いま世界が抱える7つの問題に対し、国際政治学の権威が大胆に予測！

1,500円

幸福の科学出版

大川隆法シリーズ・最新刊

日本をもう一度ブッ壊す
小泉純一郎元総理守護霊メッセージ

「ワン・フレーズ・ポリティクス」「劇場型」の小泉政治と、「アベノミクス」「安倍外交」を比較する時、現代の日本政治の問題点が浮き彫りになる。
【幸福実現党刊】

1,400円

ロシアの本音 プーチン大統領守護霊 vs. 大川裕太

日露首脳会談は、なぜ失敗に終わったのか？今回の首脳会談に対するロシア側の不満とは？トランプによって変化する米露・中露の関係とは？

1,400円

繁栄への決断
「トランプ革命」と日本の「新しい選択」

TPP、対中戦略、ロシア外交、EU危機……。「トランプ革命」によって激変する世界情勢のなか、日本の繁栄を実現する「新しい選択」とは？

1,500円

※表示価格は本体価格（税別）です。

大川隆法「法シリーズ」・**最新刊**

伝道の法

人生の「真実」に目覚める時

法シリーズ第23作

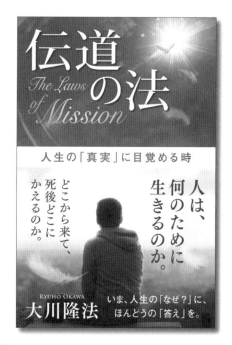

2,000円

人生の悩みや苦しみは
どうしたら解決できるのか。
世界の争いや憎しみは
どうしたらなくなるのか。
ここに、ほんとうの「答え」がある。

第1章　心の時代を生きる　──　人生を黄金に変える「心の力」
第2章　魅力ある人となるためには──批判する人をもファンに変える力
第3章　人類幸福化の原点　──　宗教心、信仰心は、なぜ大事なのか
第4章　時代を変える奇跡の力
　　　　　　　　──　危機の時代を乗り越える「宗教」と「政治」
第5章　慈悲の力に目覚めるためには
　　　　　　　　──　一人でも多くの人に愛の心を届けたい
第6章　信じられる世界へ──　あなたにも、世界を幸福に変える「光」がある

幸福の科学出版　　　　　　　　　　　　　※表示価格は本体価格(税別)です。

夏のあの日。
思い返せばわかることだった。
君のまなざしは、
すべて知っていたのだと──

君のまなざし

製作総指揮・原案／大川隆法

梅崎快人 水月ゆうこ 大川宏洋 手塚理美 黒沢年雄 黒田アーサー 日向丈 長谷川奈央 合香美希 春宮みずき
(特別出演)

監督／赤羽博 総合プロデューサー・脚本／大川宏洋 音楽／水澤有一 製作・企画／ニュースター・プロダクション 制作プロダクション／ジャンゴフィルム
配給／日活 配給協力／東京テアトル ©2017 NEW STAR PRODUCTION

2017年5月 ROADSHOW　　kimimana-movie.jp

幸福の科学グループのご案内

宗教、教育、政治、出版などの活動を通じて、地球的ユートピアの実現を目指しています。

幸福の科学

1986年に立宗。信仰の対象は、地球系霊団の最高大霊、主エル・カンターレ。世界100カ国以上の国々に信者を持ち、全人類救済という尊い使命のもと、信者は、「愛」と「悟り」と「ユートピア建設」の教えの実践、伝道に励んでいます。

(2017年1月現在)

愛

幸福の科学の「愛」とは、与える愛です。これは、仏教の慈悲(じひ)や布施(ふせ)の精神と同じことです。信者は、仏法真理をお伝えすることを通して、多くの方に幸福な人生を送っていただくための活動に励んでいます。

悟り

「悟り」とは、自らが仏の子であることを知るということです。教学(きょうがく)や精神統一によって心を磨き、智慧(ちえ)を得て悩みを解決すると共に、天使・菩薩(ぼさつ)の境地を目指し、より多くの人を救える力を身につけていきます。

ユートピア建設

私たち人間は、地上に理想世界を建設するという尊い使命を持って生まれてきています。社会の悪を押しとどめ、善を推し進めるために、信者はさまざまな活動に積極的に参加しています。

海外支援・災害支援

国内外の世界で貧困や災害、心の病で苦しんでいる人々に対しては、現地メンバーや支援団体と連携して、物心両面にわたり、あらゆる手段で手を差し伸べています。

ヘレンの会

ヘレン・ケラーを理想として活動する、ハンディキャップを持つ方とボランティアの会です。視聴覚障害者、肢体不自由な方々に仏法真理を学んでいただくための、さまざまなサポートをしています。

公式サイト www.helen-hs.net

自殺を減らそうキャンペーン

年間約3万人の自殺者を減らすため、全国各地で街頭キャンペーンを展開しています。

公式サイト www.withyou-hs.net

INFORMATION

お近くの精舎・支部・拠点など、お問い合わせは、こちらまで！
幸福の科学サービスセンター
TEL. **03-5793-1727**（受付時間 火〜金:10〜20時／土・日・祝日:10〜18時）
幸福の科学公式サイト **happy-science.jp**

幸福の科学グループの教育・人材養成事業

ハッピー・サイエンス・ユニバーシティ
Happy Science University

ハッピー・サイエンス・ユニバーシティとは

ハッピー・サイエンス・ユニバーシティ(HSU)は、大川隆法総裁が設立された「現代の松下村塾」であり、「日本発の本格私学」です。
建学の精神として「幸福の探究と新文明の創造」を掲げ、チャレンジ精神にあふれ、新時代を切り拓く人材の輩出を目指します。

学部のご案内

人間幸福学部

人間学を学び、新時代を切り拓くリーダーとなる

経営成功学部

企業や国家の繁栄を実現する、起業家精神あふれる人材となる

未来産業学部

新文明の源流を創造するチャレンジャーとなる

未来創造学部

時代を変え、未来を創る主役となる

政治家やジャーナリスト、ライター、俳優・タレントなどのスター、映画監督・脚本家などのクリエーター人材を育てます。※

※キャンパスは東京がメインとなり、2年制の短期特進課程も新設します(4年制の1年次は千葉です)。2017年3月までは、赤坂「ユートピア活動推進館」、2017年4月より東京都江東区(東西線東陽町駅近く)の新校舎「HSU未来創造・東京キャンパス」がキャンパスとなります。

住所 〒299-4325 千葉県長生郡長生村一松丙 4427-
TEL.0475-32-7770

幸福の科学グループの教育・人材養成事業

教育

学校法人 幸福の科学学園

学校法人 幸福の科学学園は、幸福の科学の教育理念のもとにつくられた教育機関です。人間にとって最も大切な宗教教育の導入を通じて精神性を高めながら、ユートピア建設に貢献する人材輩出を目指しています。

幸福の科学学園

中学校・高等学校（那須本校）
2010年4月開校・栃木県那須郡（男女共学・全寮制）
TEL 0287-75-7777
公式サイト happy-science.ac.jp

関西中学校・高等学校（関西校）
2013年4月開校・滋賀県大津市（男女共学・寮及び通学）
TEL 077-573-7774
公式サイト kansai.happy-science.ac.jp

仏法真理塾「サクセスNo.1」 TEL 03-5750-0747（東京本校）
小・中・高校生が、信仰教育を基礎にしながら、「勉強も『心の修行』」と考えて学んでいます。

不登校児支援スクール「ネバー・マインド」 TEL 03-5750-1741
心の面からのアプローチを重視して、不登校の子供たちを支援しています。
また、障害児支援の「ユー・アー・エンゼル！」運動も行っています。

エンゼルプランV TEL 03-5750-0757
幼少時からの心の教育を大切にして、信仰をベースにした幼児教育を行っています。

シニア・プラン21 TEL 03-6384-0778
希望に満ちた生涯現役人生のために、年齢を問わず、多くの方が学んでいます。

NPO活動支援

学校からのいじめ追放を目指し、さまざまな社会提言をしています。また、各地でのシンポジウムや学校への啓発ポスター掲示等に取り組む一般財団法人「いじめから子供を守ろうネットワーク」を支援しています。

ブログ blog.mamoro.org
公式サイト mamoro.org
相談窓口 TEL.03-5719-2170

幸福の科学グループ事業

政治

幸福実現党

内憂外患(ないゆうがいかん)の国難に立ち向かうべく、2009年5月に幸福実現党を立党しました。創立者である大川隆法党総裁の精神的指導のもと、宗教だけでは解決できない問題に取り組み、幸福を具体化するための力になっています。

幸福実現党 釈量子サイト
shaku-ryoko.net

Twitter
釈量子@shakuryoko
で検索

党の機関紙
「幸福実現NEWS」

幸福実現党 党員募集中

あなたも幸福を実現する政治に参画しませんか。

○ 幸福実現党の理念と綱領、政策に賛同する18歳以上の方なら、どなたでも党員になることができます。
○ 党員の期間は、党費(年額 一般党員5,000円、学生党員2,000円)を入金された日から1年間となります。

党員になると

党員限定の機関紙が送付されます(学生党員の方にはメールにてお送りします)。
申込書は、下記、幸福実現党公式サイトでダウンロードできます。

住所 〒107-0052
東京都港区赤坂2-10-8 6階
幸福実現党本部

TEL 03-6441-0754
FAX 03-6441-0764
公式サイト hr-party.jp
若者向け政治サイト truthyouth.jp

幸福の科学グループ事業

出版メディア事業

アー・ユー・ハッピー?
are-you-happy.com

ザ・リバティ
the-liberty.com

幸福の科学出版

大川隆法総裁の仏法真理の書を中心に、ビジネス、自己啓発、小説など、さまざまなジャンルの書籍・雑誌を出版しています。他にも、映画事業、文学・学術発展のための振興事業、テレビ・ラジオ番組の提供など、幸福の科学文化を広げる事業を行っています。

幸福の科学出版
TEL 03-5573-7700
公式サイト irhpress.co.jp

ザ・ファクト
マスコミが報道しない「事実」を世界に伝えるネット・オピニオン番組

Youtubeにて随時好評配信中!

ザ・ファクト　検索

ニュースター・プロダクション

ニュースター・プロダクション(株)は、新時代の"美しさ"を創造する芸能プロダクションです。2016年3月には、映画「天使に"アイム・ファイン"」を公開。2017年初夏には、ニュースター・プロダクション企画の映画「君のまなざし」を公開予定です。

公式サイト newstarpro.co.jp

ニュースター・プリンセス・オーディション

ニュースター・プロダクションは、2018年公開予定映画のヒロイン人材を求めて、全国規模のオーディションを開催します。あなたも映画のヒロインを目指して、応募してみませんか?

詳しくはこちら　ニュースター・プロダクション　検索

入会のご案内

あなたも、幸福の科学に集い、ほんとうの幸福を見つけてみませんか?

幸福の科学では、大川隆法総裁が説く仏法真理をもとに、「どうすれば幸福になれるのか、また、他の人を幸福にできるのか」を学び、実践しています。

大川隆法総裁の教えを信じ、学ぼうとする方なら、どなたでも入会できます。入会された方には、『入会版「正心法語」』が授与されます。(入会の奉納は1,000円目安です)

ネットでも入会できます。詳しくは、下記URLへ。
happy-science.jp/joinus

仏弟子としてさらに信仰を深めたい方は、仏・法・僧の三宝への帰依を誓う「三帰誓願式」を受けることができます。三帰誓願者には、『仏説・正心法語』『祈願文①』『祈願文②』『エル・カンターレへの祈り』が授与されます。

三帰誓願(さんきせいがん)

植福の会(しょくふくのかい)

植福は、ユートピア建設のために、自分の富を差し出す尊い布施の行為です。布施の機会として、毎月1口1,000円からお申込みいただける、「植福の会」がございます。

ご希望の方には、幸福の科学の小冊子(毎月1回)をお送りいたします。詳しくは、下記の電話番号までお問い合わせください。

月刊「幸福の科学」　ザ・伝道　ヤング・ブッダ　ヘルメス・エンゼルズ　What's 幸福の科学

INFORMATION
幸福の科学サービスセンター
TEL. 03-5793-1727 (受付時間 火~金:10~20時/土・日・祝日:10~18時)
幸福の科学 公式サイト **happy-science.jp**